WHY YOU SHC

A TREE GROWS IN . . .

There is a Tree that has its r‹

This Tree contains all that is   l
could be. It contains a Kingdom, a ɪ ouɪ̣ɑ── ,   ,
Beauty, Might, Mercy, Understanding, . . . and a Crown.

A Tree of *Knowledge*? More . . . **The Tree of Life!** It is the system
known as the "Mystical (and by some as the 'Magical') Qabala".

It contains a system for training the mind, making proper astral contacts, guiding spiritual growth, and more. With step-by-step procedures, with self-development exercises, with time-proven symbolism
and methods.

On this Tree . . . *in* this Tree . . . are Meditations that can, properly
applied, **bring about *specific* spiritual experiences**, solve problems,
provide answers . . . with practical as well as spiritual benefit.

On this Tree may be found Deity — as Creative Power, as the Ancient
of Ancients, as the Goddess in all Her Beauty and the God in all His
Strengths, as all the Gods and Powers (by whatever name) that have
ever been and ever will be. Through this Tree, we may experience
The Mysteries, find our way through The Labyrinth, and traverse
The Path.

The Qabala is a complete system for organizing your experience of
the Universe and to gain understanding of the various levels of existence from the most abstract to the most concrete, and to give the
means (the Knowledge and the Power) to do specific *magic* — whether
spiritual or mundane — to make desired changes in your life.

This book is unique: it is written for people who have neither the
interest nor the background in the Qabala's Jewish origins or its
Christian and Masonic interpretations. It makes it possible to understand and use the Qabalistic System without dependence upon
scholarship or facility with ancient languages, and to work within
the framework of modern pagan beliefs: those who seek to return to
close harmony with the Earth and with All Life, who find Divinity
within Body and Soul and in the Earth and the Sky, who look for
Truth wherever it may be found, accepting responsibility for their
own Destiny.

THIS TREE GROWS IN *YOU*, . . . for the Qabala is a system for
perfecting the Universe that is within as without, to achieve Unity
and the Completion that is your hidden purpose in this life.

About the Author

Ellen Cannon Reed, High Priestess of the Isian tradition, has been student and teacher of the Craft and Qabala for fifteen years. She and her husband (and High Priest), Chris, have been active in the Southern California pagan community for the last ten years. They live on a hill overlooking the San Fernando Valley. When she's not teaching, working with her coven or writing, Ellen enjoys embroidery, beadwork and reading.

To Write to the Author

If you wish to contact the author or would like more information about this book, please write to the author in care of Llewellyn Worldwide, and we will forward you request. Both the author and publisher appreciate hearing from you and learning of your enjoyment of this book and how it has helped you. Llewellyn Worldwide cannot guarantee that every letter written to the author can be answered, but all will be forwarded. Please write to:

Ellen Cannon Reed
c/o Llewellyn Worldwide
P.O. Box 64383-666, St. Paul, MN 55164-0383, U.S.A.

Please enclose a self-addressed, stamped envelope for reply,
or $1.00 to cover costs.
If outside the U.S.A., enclose international postal reply coupon.

Free Catalog from Llewellyn

For more than 90 years Llewellyn has brought its readers knowledge in the fields of metaphysics and human potential. Learn about the newest books in spiritual guidance, natural healing, astrology, occult philosophy and more. Enjoy book reviews, new age articles, a calendar of events, plus current advertised products and services. To get your free copy of *Llewellyn's New Worlds of Mind and Spirit*, send your name and address to:

Llewellyn's New Worlds of Mind and Spirit
P.O. Box 64383-666, St. Paul, MN 55164-0383, U.S.A.

ABOUT LLEWELLYN'S MODERN WITCHCRAFT SERIES

Witchcraft is a word derived from an older word, *Wicca* or *Wicce*. The older word means "to bend" or "wise." Thus, those who practiced Wicca were those who followed the path of the Wise. Those who practiced the craft of the Wicca were able to bend reality to their desires: they could do magic.

Today, Witchcraft is different from what it was eons ago. Witchcraft is no longer robes and secret rites. As the Aquarian Age—the New Age—approaches fruition, the mystical secrets of the past are being made public. The result is a set of spiritual and magical systems with which anyone can feel comfortable. Modern Witchcraft—Wicca—may be the path for you!

Llewellyn's Modern Witchcraft Series of books will not only present the secrets of the Craft of the Wise so that anyone can use them, but will also share successful techniques that are working for Witches throughout the world. This will include philosophies and techniques that at one time were considered foreign to "the Craft," but are now being incorporated by modern Wiccans into their beliefs and procedures.

However, the core of Wicca will stay the same—that is the nature of Witchcraft. All of the books in this series will be practical and easy to use. They will all show a love of nature and a love of the Goddess as well as respect for the Masculine Force. You will find that this series of books is deeply rooted in spirituality, peacefulness and love.

These books will focus on Wicca and Wiccans today, not what was done a hundred, a thousand or ten thousand years ago. They will help you to expand your horizons and achieve your goals. We invite you to follow this series and look toward the future of what some have called the fastest growing religion in the world, a religion that is personal, non-judgemental and non-institutional, natural and magical—that brings forth the experience of the sacredness of ALL Life. Witchcraft is called "the Old Religion" and it is found present in the oldest myths and artifacts of humanity. This series will help you see what it will develop into tomorrow.

Also by Ellen Cannon Reed

The Witches Tarot: The Witches Qabala, Book 2
The Witches Tarot Deck (with Martin Cannon)
Invocation of the Gods

Llewellyn's Modern Witchcraft Series

The Goddess and the Tree

(formerly *The Witches' Qabala*)

The Witches Qabala
Book I

Ellen Cannon Reed

1993
Llewellyn Publications
St. Paul, Minnesota 55164-0383, U.S.A.

SECOND EDITION, REVISED
Third Printing, 1993

Cover art by Martin Cannon

Library of Congress Cataloging-in-Publication Data
Reed, Ellen Cannon, 1943-
    The witches Qabala.

    (bk. 2: Llewellyn's modern witchcraft series)
    Includes bibliographies and indexes.
    Contents: Bk. 1. The goddess and the tree—
Bk. 2. The witches tarot.
    1. Cabala. I. Title. II. Series: Llewellyn's modern
witchcraft series.
BF1611.R43   1985   135'.4   84-48088
ISBN 0-87542-666-2 (pbk. : bk. 1)
ISBN 0-87542-668-9 (bk. 2)

Llewellyn Publications
A Division of Llewellyn Worldwide, Ltd.
P.O. 64383, St. Paul, MN 55164-0383

ACKNOWLEDGMENTS

My thanks and appreciation to Karen Charbonneau and Jim and Susan Davis, who helped me with my Celtic attributions, and to the other Pacific Circle pagans who wanted to read a book about Qabala for pagans.

ACKNOWLEDGMENTS

DEDICATION

To Margo, who gave me the torch to carry,
and
To Christopher, husband, best friend and aim-crier

PREFACE

My coven training contained the usual subjects—ritual, herbology, the seasons, astrology, spell-casting and Qabala. It wasn't until much later that I discovered Qabala was not only an unusual subject in Craft training, but was shunned by many as an unsuitable subject for any pagan tradition. The subject was my favorite, and what I considered my most valuable tool was a no-no for my fellow pagans. Why?

I started re-reading my books on Qabala and discovered why: All these books were written by ceremonial magicians or Christian Qabalists who not only didn't write *for* pagans, but worded their books in such a way as to alienate those with beliefs similar to mine. It was probably not deliberate, but that was the result. I had not been alienated because I was so involved in my subject, I passed right over such passages. Someone new to Qabala and unsure of the subject would be easily offended.

Pagans were missing the value of Qabala because of the way the information was worded, and that seemed a horrible waste to me.

I presented a lecture on Qabala for Pagans and the reaction of the audience confirmed my beliefs that Qabala was acceptable to paganfolk if presented correctly. I am attempting such a presentation here.

As I write, I am trying to imagine who you are, my readers. My imagination presents me with the following groups:

- Students of the occult (Craft and Qabala) who are studying with a teacher.
- Solitary students who do not have a teacher either by choice or from lack of opportunity.
- Qabalists who (a) are wondering what the hell business a witch has writing about Qabala and are horrified at the whole idea, or (b) are delighted to see the Qabala made available to more people.
- Teachers, group leaders, High Priests and High Priestesses, etc. of pagan groups (covens, groves, etc.), seekers who have not yet found their path.
- All the rest of you.

To the last group — Blessed be!

To the penultimate group, I will you success in your search, for the finding of your proper path is a singularly joyful discovery. The Craft is a lovely path, though not for everyone. If you find, as you read, that you relate to the ideas reflected here, are drawn to a path that reveres life and recognizes both Lord and Lady, I suggest you read *Spiral Dance* by Starhawk, and *Witchcraft, the Sixth Sense*, by Justine Glass. Whatever your way may be, there is material here that can be of use to you.

To the first group — students with a teacher, I don't believe there is anything here which could interfere with what you are being taught, but it would be courteous to discuss it with your teacher. Better yet, lend them this book and *then* discuss it.

To the solitaries by choice: Greetings, and I hope you find this word useful.

To the other solitaries: good luck in finding a teacher. Methods of doing so are included here.

To the teachers: In my own experience as High Priestess, I've found Qabala an invaluable help. With it, you can guide your students toward direct spiritual experience, understand, provide help for and even predict specific problems, and you can use the Qabala to contact specific energies for your rituals. All this is in addition to the help it can provide in your own spiritual work.

To my fellow Qabalists who are in favor of my work, thank you for your support, and Blessed be!

To the Qabalist who is about to strike me with lightning—my, what an intolerant, narrow attitude you have! If ancient Qabalists had had your attitude, the study would never have grown past the original glyph. The Tree of Life holds all of Creation and more. Surely there is room for different points of view.

To all the rest, greetings!

I have tried to keep all of you in mind as I wrote, although the book is aimed at paganfolk.

I have not attempted to write a definitive book on Qabala. In a lifetime or two I might, but not here, not now. What I have tried to do is create a bridge to the Qabala, to introduce you to the subject in such a way that you will see its value and will be able to pursue its study without being alienated.

There is plenty to work with in this book alone, but I hope you'll study further, seek out the recommended books. If you are intrigued enough to do that, I will be content. If you go even further and decide to make Qabala part of your spiritual work and/or include it in the studies of your group, I will be delighted.

The Charge of the Goddess

Listen to the words of the Great Mother, who was of old called amongst men, Isis, Artemis, Astarte, Dione, Melusine, Aphrodite, Diana, Arionrhod, and by many other names.

Whenever you have need of anything, once in the month and better it be when the Moon is full or new, then shall ye assemble in some secret place and adore the spirit of Me, Queen of all Witcheries. There shall ye assemble, who have not yet won my deepest secrets and are fain to learn all sorceries. To these shall I teach that which is as yet unknown. Ye shall be free from all slavery, and as a sign that you be free, ye shall be naked in your rites. You shall sing, feast, make music and love, all in my presence, for Mine is the ecstasy of the spirit, and mine is also joy upon earth. My law is love unto all beings. Mine is the Secret that opens upon the door of youth, and mine is the cup of the wine of life, the cauldron of Cerridwen, which is the Holy Grail of Immortality. I am the Gracious Goddess who gives the gift of youth unto the heart of mankind. I give knowledge of the Spirit Eternal, and beyond death, I give peace and freedom and reunion with those who have gone before. Nor do I demand aught of sacrifice, for behold, I am the Mother of all things and my love is poured out upon the Earth.

Hear ye the words of the Star Goddess, She, in the dust of whose feet are the hosts of heaven, whose body encircles the universe.

I am the beauty of the Green Earth, and the White Moon among the stars and the mystery of the Waters. I call unto thy soul: Arise and come unto me. For I am the Soul of Nature who gives life to the universe: from me all things proceed and unto me all things return. Beloved of all the Gods and men, let my worship be in the heart. Rejoice, for behold, all acts of love and pleasure are my rituals. Therefore, let there be beauty and strength—power and compassion—honor and humility—mirth and reverence within you. And you who think to seek me, know that your seeking and yearning will avail you not, unless you know the Mystery, that if that which you seek you find not within yourself, you will never find it without. For behold, I have been with you from the beginning, and I am that which is attained at the end of desire.

from the traditional Charge

I seek the Crown
of Wisdom and Understanding
That Might and Mercy
In balance bring Beauty.
Victory and Glory
Find their Foundation
In the Kingdom.

TABLE OF CONTENTS

CHAPTER 1
THE MYSTERIES OF THE WEST 1
Legendary history of the Qabala. How it came into
non-Hebrew magical works. How it can relate to
paganism.

CHAPTER 2
THE TREE OF LIFE 7
The glyph known as the Tree of Life, what it is and
its various correspondences.

CHAPTER 3
"I AM THAT WHICH IS ATTAINED AT THE END
OF DESIRE" 17
Kether, the sphere of creation. The beginning and the
end.

CHAPTER 4
"I HAVE BEEN WITH THEE FROM THE
BEGINNING" 21
Chokmah, the sphere of the God, the Father, the idea
of Force.

CHAPTER 5
"LISTEN TO THE WORDS OF THE
GREAT MOTHER". 27
Binah, the sphere of the Goddess, the Mother, the idea
of Form.

CHAPTER 6
"THERE SHALL YE ASSEMBLE" 33
Chesed, the sphere of the Ancient Ones, of order and
building.

CHAPTER 7
"AND YE SHALL BE FREE . . . ." 37
Geburah, the sphere of Karma, of cutting away.

CHAPTER 8
LET THERE BE BEAUTY 45
Tifareth, the sphere of harmony, of giving, the sphere
of the sun, and illumination.

CHAPTER 9

"FOR BEHOLD, ALL ACTS OF LOVE AND PLEASURE
ARE MY RITUALS"................................51
Netzach, the sphere of emotion, of love in all forms,
of creativity, and the arts.

CHAPTER 10

"TO THESE SHALL I TEACH THAT WHICH IS AS YET
UNKNOWN"....................................57
Hod, the sphere of learning, of science and books,
of words and ritual.

CHAPTER 11

"... AND THE WHITE MOON AMONG THE STARS".....63
Yesod, the sphere of the Moon, the Astral Plane.

CHAPTER 12

"I AM THE BEAUTY OF THE GREEN EARTH".........71
Malkuth, the sphere of manifestation, of all that is
physical.

CHAPTER 13

THE FOUR WORLDS 77
The four types of energy represented by the four
worlds of the spheres.

CHAPTER 14

CREATING YOUR OWN TREE 81
Making your own Tree of Life for Magical use.

CHAPTER 15

"THOU WHO THINKEST TO SEEK ME".............87
The use of the Qabala for solitary and personal
work, the problems involved in working without a
teacher, some exercises and meditations.

CHAPTER 16

QABALA FOR TEACHERS AND GROUPS............101
Using the Qabala to understand the growth of students and their problems, using the Vices and Virtues
to recognize stages of growth, types of group work
using the Qabala.

CHAPTER 17

    CONCLUSION 111
        The Qabala as it appears in everyday life, its values
        and uses.

APPENDIX I

    THE SPHERES AND THEIR CORRESPONDENCES. 115

APPENDIX II

    THE ASTRAL TEMPLES 127

APPENDIX III

    THE SPHERES IN MAGICAL WORK. 135
        Which spere to use for what.

APPENDIX IV

    PRONUNCIATION GUIDE. 137

APPENDIX V

    THE SHARED CROSS. 139
        A form of the Qabalistic Cross to be used as a sharing
        between members of circles.

APPENDIX VI

    THE RITE OF MENDING LOVE. 143
        A ritual using both pagan and Qabalistic symbolism.

RECOMMENDED READING 149

BIBLIOGRAPHY 151

INDEX 153

ILLUSTRATIONS

The Tree of Life with Hebrew Names .8

The Tree of Life on the Pillars 9

The Tree of Life with English Names. 18

Deities on the Tree 22

Names of Power on the Tree 26

Archangels on the Tree. 32

Angels on the Tree (Hebrew Names) .38

Angels on the Tree (English Names) .46

Planetary Attributions 52

Spiritual Experiences 56

Perfumes 62

Precious and Semi-precious Stones 70

Animals on the Tree. 78

Colors on the Tree. 82

The Paths on the Tree 86

The Tarot on the Tree 95

Virtues of Each Sphere. 102

Vices of Each Sphere 105

Elemental Circles. 112

Temple of Malkuth 128

Temple of Yesod. 130

Temple of Hod 131

Temple of Netzach 133

The Circle Shared Cross 140

Altar Arrangement for Rite. 144

CHAPTER 1

THE MYSTERIES OF THE WEST

Beginning in the late 19th century, a great interest in the Eastern philosophies was born in the West. In the days preceding and during a tremendous growth in scientific knowledge, in industry and in later years a reach for outer space, many developed an interest in their "inner space" and yearned for something not provided by the religions they had inherited.

Psychology and psychiatry had begun their exploration of the human mind, and even members of that august fraternity, most notably Carl Gustave Jung, realized that the conscious mind was only a small part of a true inner self, in spite of the inclination of the scientific community to accept only that which could be proven "scientifically".

The Eastern philosophies did offer an understanding of that self, a contact with it, and many people found comfort and a measure of peace in what was offered. Madame Blavatsky and her fellow Theosophists were among the first to introduce these ideas (albeit somewhat mixed with various Western ideologies) to the West. In the 1960's, this interest experienced a re-birth, spurred by their adoption by many well-known figures.

However, as so many discovered, the differences between the East and West are numerous, not the least of which is a vast difference in attitude and culture. We are not of the same "mind-set", and the Oriental philosophy of withdrawal from life is not practical in a world where that withdrawal must contend with the hurry-scurry, make-a-living, do-it-now atmosphere we of the West live in. We needed something different, a *Western* esoteric philosophy, suitable to *our* way of life.

Such a philosophy, in fact several of them, have existed for many years, some since before the Christian era. Those of us who have found our way to the Craft of the Wise Ones (Witchcraft) and other similar beliefs know this; we live one of them. Our path is one which reveres a Heavenly Mother as well as a Heavenly Father, cherishes all that lives, accepts Divinity within ourselves as well as without, and embraces the belief in reincarnation.

There are others, and we are fortunate to live in an age when information on all the magical paths is so easily available. We are no longer restricted to the knowledge inherited and developed by our own small groups; we are in contact with other traditions; we learn and share and grow. Techniques, tools, methods, knowledge from others have added to our lives and our spirituality. One source of these is the Qabala.

The obvious question for one new to the Qabala is of course, "What is it?" Turning to the authors most qualified in this strange and mysterious subject, we find the following: W. G. Gray calls it "symbolic representations of the relationship believed to exist between the most abstract divinity and the most concrete humanity". He also calls it "a family tree linking God and man together with angels and other beings as a complete conscious creation". Dion Fortune defines Qabala as "an attempt to reduce to diagrammatic form every force and factor in the manifested universe and the soul of man; to correlate them to one another and reveal them spread out as on a map so that the relative positions between them can be seen and the relations between them traced . . . a compendium of science, psychology, philosophy and theology".

Somewhat more simply, Israel Regardie says, "The Qabala is a trustworthy guide, leading to a comprehension both of the Universe and one's own Self". From Gareth Knight we hear, "A practical method for the interrelations of various systems of symbols". It has been called a framework, a stepladder for spiritual growth, and a tool for the study of comparative religion. A. LaDage calls it "a system for obtaining direct religious experience. From W. E. Butler comes "a method of using the mind in a practical and constantly widening consideration of the Universal soul of man".

The Qabala is all of these, and more. My own favorite definition, to paraphrase Dr. Regardie, is "a file cabinet to contain the Universe". That may sound frivolous, but it is not, nor is it inaccurate. The Qabala provides a filing cabinet for the mind, giving you a place for everything. Even better, the Qabala offers you a retrieval system, not only for information *you* have placed in this cabinet, but eventually for information placed there over the centuries by other practitioners of Qabalism. The Qabala is a way of tying all your studies together, relating them to each other, enabling you to understand each more completely.

It is also a tool that can be used to guide your personal growth, and to measure it. It can be used for personal and for group work, by solitary, student and teacher. And, while it is not effective after a quick glance at the material, it is not at all difficult to use. In the following chapters, you will find information that can be put to use immediately.

How can a philosophy attributed to a patriarchal, monotheistic religion possible relate to a polytheistic, matriarchal religion? Not only does the Qabala relate well to paganism, but the mystical Qabala relates better, in my opinion, to the beliefs of paganism than it does to modern Judaism. Qabala recognizes the feminine in Deity in other words, the Goddess, as a vital part of the energies of the Universe. It was because of this recognition that Qabala was proclaimed heresy by orthodox Jews at one point in history, and even today is not well-thought-of by many Jews.

At present, I'm told that Qabala is not taught to anyone under the age of 35 unless they are married. The age limit could reflect a desire for maturity in students, but I'm at a loss to understand how being married could qualify you. Perhaps the modern Hebrew teachers have found something a lot racier than I have in this subject.

This recognition of the Goddess is the first point in favor of the Qabala, as our spiritual ancestors discovered long ago.

The word "Qabala" comes from a Hebrew word QBL (Qoph Beth Lamed), "to receive". In ancient Hebrew, there were no written vowels until approximately 700 A.D., so when transliterated to our alphabet, "a" was placed in as the nearest sound. This transliteration accounts for the varied spellings of the word: Kabbalah, Qabalah, etc. You are free to choose the spelling you prefer.

Legend has it that Qabala was given to ancient Hebrew scholars by an archangel for the purpose of helping them to experience the Mysteries, and to help others experience them. I deliberately did not say "teach the Mysteries", for by definition, Mysteries are those "received" teachings which cannot be taught. Only the glyph known as the Tree of Life and the Names of Power were given to the ancients. All other correspondences have been added since.

Another version of the legend holds that the Qabala was given to Moses on Sinai, at the same time he was given the Ten Commandments. Moses passed this knowledge on to Joshua who passed it on to the Judges, who passed it on as they saw fit.

If the Qabala did come from (through) Moses, it is worthwhile to consider his upbringing. He was raised as an Egyptian prince, and probably trained as a priest in the Egyptian Mysteries. It is therefore possible that much of that training and those mysteries are incorporated into the Qabala.

It matters not. It does not even matter if, as some skeptics contend, the Qabala was pieced together by Moses de Leon in the twelfth century. It is valid. It works, that is what is truly important, and it works today in our world, in our culture, our way of life, our religion. It is a living system, a growing one, ancient and ever new.

During the first centuries after Christ, when the Church was growing in power, the Jewish religion was considered as pagan as other pre-Christian religions, and all were forced underground together. No doubt there was a great deal of sharing and interchange between members of these faiths, and it is very probably at this time that non-Hebrew scholars became aware of the Qabala, recognized its value, and blithely appropriated it for their own. My teacher once told me, "A good witch is eclectic. She'll steal anything that works". In the search for spiritual understanding, this is a usual thing, and rightly so.

The Qabala began to develop in a new way. We added planetary attributions, the Tarot, Gods and Goddesses, jewels, animals, elements, plants and a multitude of other correspondences to the Tree. These additions have taken place over the centuries, and are taking place today. It is of this Qabala that I speak, the magical or mystical Qabala.

The Tree has grown and flowered since its introduction to humanity. It has been filled with ideas, with spiritual experience, with the effort and hearts and energy of hundreds of thousands of its users, with so much that we can use and benefit from. It is here for you to learn from and for you to contribute to. The study of the Qabala, the adoption of it into your life, your thoughts, puts you in touch with knowledge placed there by those who have gone before, our elder brethren, by their adoption and use of this magical mystical tool.

CHAPTER 2

THE TREE OF LIFE

The first and largest step in showing you the value of the Qabala is to explain, in small part, the significance of the glyph known as the Tree of Life. As shown on the diagram, the glyph consists of ten spheres, joined by 22 "paths". These spheres, "sephiroth" in Hebrew, are arranged in three triangles with the tenth sphere hanging below the other nine. These spheres and the paths that join them are the "file drawers" of this universal file cabinet.

The study of Qabala involves, among other things, the study of the meanings of these spheres, and their relationships to each other. One aspect of this study is the arrangement of the spheres into "pillars", the spheres on the left of the tree being in one pillar, those in the center in another, and those on the right in a third.

Traditionally, these pillars are called (from left to right) the Feminine Pillar, the Middle Pillar, and the Masculine Pillar, or, the Pillar of Severity, the Pillar of Mildness or Equilibrium, and the Pillar of Mercy.

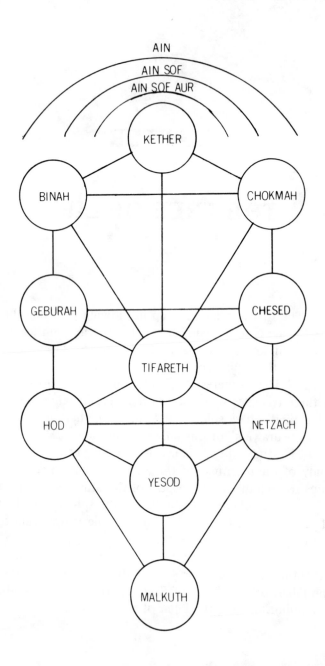

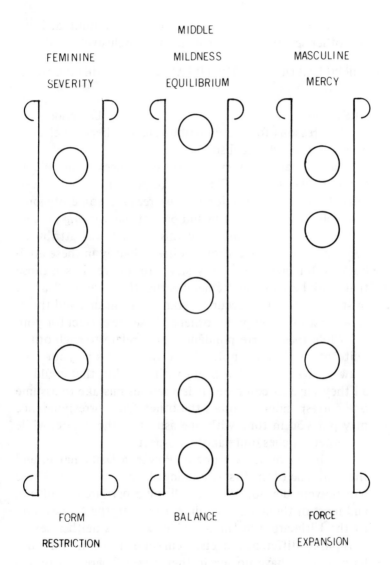

THE PILLARS

Both sets of titles are appropriate, but limited. I use two other sets of titles which are more inclusive.

THE PILLAR OF	THE PILLAR OF	THE PILLAR OF
Form		Force
or	Balance	or
Restriction		Expansion

The reasons for these attributions will become clear as we study the individual spheres.

Each sphere has various correspondences — file folders for the file drawers. These correspondences have been related to the spheres for various reasons; some obvious, some obscure. Half the fun and part of the learning process is trying to understand why this or that was attributed here or there. Each authority differs slightly in these attributions, but many are fairly standard. I have chosen those that work best for me. Remember that these are not "carved in stone". If others occur to you, by all means add them. If, after study, you prefer others, those are correct for you.

While these correspondences may relate to each other, quite often they do not. All the file folders in your "A" drawer have names that begin with "A" but that could be all they have in common. It is a serious mistake to assume one correspondence equals the other. One correspondence may put you in tune with one aspect of the sphere, while the other touches quite another aspect.

Each sphere has a Name of Power, a Deity name, and these are one of the first stumbling blocks for pagans. These names were developed, after all, by a patriarchal culture, and most of them are masculine. However, the Names refer to the Ultimate, the Unknowable, which is neither sex or both, in its different aspects, so in spite of their literal translations, they have no sex in themselves. There *is* a reason for not simply doing away with them. An attempt has been made to provide alternate translations which express the aspect represented, but that is not really necessary. Simply consider the names as those "barbarous names of evocation" we are so often accused of using. They are nothing more or less than sounds, vibratory rates which, whatever their literal meaning, can be used to tune you in to the wave length of the sphere in question. Their translation is unimportant. Their effect in use is not.

Perhaps the most useful correspondence, one that can be used from the very start, is the Magical Image. These are pictures designed to represent the sphere and the energy it signifies. Like so many magical things, these have been used by so many, so often and with such concentration that they have developed a power of their own. They work both ways: Meditation on a sphere can bring these images to mind, even if you do not know what the Magical Image should be; and, meditation on these images can put you in contact with the energies of the sphere you represent.

If you're interested in performing an experiment, after you have finished this chapter spend some time meditating on the following: "A young queen, crowned and throned". Make notes on the ideas that come to you.

As you may be beginning to see, this is not just a two-dimensional diagram. The Tree of Life is a living tree. It can be used to experience and understand the universe from deep inside you to the farthest reaches of the most abstract divinity.

There is a Planetary Attribution for each sphere, sometimes called a "mundane chakra". These are astrological figures whose significance will help those of you with an astrological background to understand further the sphere to which they are attributed, or conversely, to help those of you without an astrological background to understand further the significance of the planet. The powers represented by these figures are one of the "Four Worlds" of the Qabala.

For most spheres there is a Vice and a Virtue . . . reactions to the energy of a sphere as it begins to have an effect on a human being. Humans being imperfect vehicles, (at this stage of our development) the negative reaction or Vice, usually manifests itself first. Hopefully, this will purify into the positive reaction, or Virtue.

The Vice and Virtue are also indications of the amount of that particular energy present. The right amount will show the positive aspect; an imbalance or overflow, the negative.

Dion Fortune expresses all of the above by saying that the virtue is the result of spiritual initiation into a particular sphere.

Each Sphere has a Pagan Mythology attached to it; Deities and mythological figures that correspond to that sphere. This is one of the ways in which Qabala can be used in the study of comparative religion. If we know that Ptah can be attributed to a specific sphere, and that Brahma is attributed to the same sphere, we understand both a little better. Various Deities are attributed to more than one sphere, this designation depending on different aspects of that Deity.

I have attempted, out of respect for the Celtic traditions of the Craft, to add the Celtic pantheon to these attributions. In doing so, I differ in several instances from others who have done the same. None of these differences imply that one is right and the other wrong. As in all pantheons, the Celtic Deities are multi-faceted and can appear in several spheres. You may disagree entirely with my attributions. Good! It proves you are thinking!

We come to what I consider the most important correspondence, the SPIRITUAL EXPERIENCE, usually called "A Vision of . . . " something or other. The term "vision" is a bit misleading. These are not blinding flashes of Gods and Goddesses appearing before you, no "St. Paul on the road to Damascus" experiences. They are types of understanding, of awareness. The realization that you *have* this awareness can come in a blinding flash, but the awareness has been growing and developing within you, day by day, slowly, until you become aware of your awareness. You know that you know, and that you *have* known for some time.

These experiences, so meaningful, so important, so glorious, are also a source of frustration because they cannot be shared. You can't give them to someone. You can talk for hours and hours, and it will not help them to understand if they haven't had the experience — and no words are necessary if they have. These are the Mysteries, those things which cannot be taught, the "received teachings" which must be experienced to be learned.

If I say to you, "The Universe is a safe place. You cannot truly be harmed. And there is a plan, a pattern to it all. Things are as they should be. I know that to be true. I know it for a certainty". There are those who will agree, will understand, will nod. To those I say, "Have you ever tried to convince anyone?" It can't be done, unless the other person has had the experience known as "The Vision of the Machinery of the Universe". If they have, there is no need to convince them, they know.

Here is one of the areas where Qabala is a blessing to teachers. You cannot *teach* these awarenesses, but by using the Qabala, you can guide students toward them. Within the Qabala you'll find material for meditations, exercises, rituals that will lead them not only toward specific spiritual experience, but also to help for other specific problems, mundane or spiritual.

"Perfumes", (incenses) are found for each sephira. These can be used to accompany meditation or ritual work to help you even further in tuning in to the proper energy. That's what working with the Qabala is, tuning your mind to a specific wave length. The Tree of Life shows you where the "station" is, and you use meditation or ritual to tune in.

Although it is not really a correspondence, the information on each sphere is accompanied by a quote from the *Sepher Yetzirah*, an ancient book on Qabala. These quotations can be both informative and obscure, and are excellent sources for meditation.

Various precious stones and semi-precious stones, animals, plants, etc. are attributed to each of the sephiroth. Like the perfume, these can be used to add effect to magical workings.

Each sphere has four colors attributed to it, one for each of the Four Worlds of the Qabala. These worlds are discussed briefly in another chapter.

There is an archangel assigned to each sephira, as well as a "choir" of angels. Do not confuse angels and archangels of the Qabala with the winged angelic images you may be used to. Angels are beings (or forms of energy) created for special and precise purposes. They are capable of their own specialties, "divine robots" so to speak.

Archangels are more versatile than angels. They are the "supervisors" if you will, although that is a very simplistic way to describe such mighty and holy beings.

They are, at present, more highly evolved than humans, but angels and archangels are at the peak of their evolution. They will always be as they are. Humankind, however, will one day surpass them and rejoin our source, the God and Goddess. We are currently in the situation of a college student who will one day be Dean of the College. Whatever his future status, while he is a student, he has to listen to his teachers.

Angels and archangels are sexless, though I usually use the masculine pronoun when referring to one of the archangels. It seems more polite than "it".

The spheres have both English and Hebrew names, and various alternate titles which attempt to express their meanings, their beings.

Many of the attributions will make perfect sense to you at first reading. Others will not. Don't worry if you don't comprehend everything at once. Some day when you're puttering around, everything will come together in your mind and you will have what is known as the "mystical AHA! experience". You'll understand.

There are twenty-two paths connecting the spheres. Think of the paths as states of becoming, while the spheres are states of being. The study of the paths is an interesting one, but we will not delve too deeply into that study in this book. A few paths will be discussed briefly.

There is a "Tree of Evil" said to be below the Tree of Life. I don't feel this has a part in the Craft beliefs and well may be a later and unnecessary addition to the Qabala.

You will find no "evil" energies in this book, although the energies represented by the spheres of the Tree can be used in ways which bring harm to others. It is possible to learn some control of these powers without the spiritual development that should accompany that knowledge.

It is *not* possible to harm others without ultimately bringing harm to yourself, for we are all one, and what we do to others we are doing to ourselves. To harm ourselves, even indirectly, is stupid at the very least. Ideally, the person who would commit such an act is to be pitied, and perhaps souls of a more advanced state than mine can actually feel that pity. Those who do harm will learn, painfully, and their lessons all the more painful for the harm they have inflicted.

Have you ever looked back on a small cruelty you committed as a child and regretted it? Children are not deliberately cruel, but they do not understand that other children are "real". Empathy and sympathy come with maturity.

Black magic is only done by those who do not understand that other people are part of themselves, that "what's going out is what's coming in".

It is very easy to say, almost as easy to accept, and very difficult to sympathize with those who commit harmful acts. Nevertheless, it is what we should feel. If you remember what you felt when you recalled your childhood cruelties — how much greater will be the anguish they feel when they realize what they've done.

There are other aspects in the study of the Qabala that we will not deal with in this book. These are *temura, gematria* and *notaricon*. All these are methods of searching for hidden meanings, especially in the Old Testament.

Temura is related to modern cryptography. The addition, subtraction and substitution of letters in words, or reading them in different orders are among its methods.

Notaricon has many modern practitioners, for it deals with acronyms, taking the first (and sometimes last) letters of a sentence and creating a word which signifies the whole sentence. Two modern examples of notaricon are "laser" (Light Amplification by the Stimulated Emission of Radiation) and "radar" (Radio Detecting And Ranging).

Gematria is the numerology of the Qabala. Each letter in the Hebrew alphabet also represents a number. Gematrists believe the words that have the same number have the same meaning.

If these interest you, information can be found in other books.

Let us move on to a study of the individual spheres and how they may be useful to you.

CHAPTER 3

"I AM THAT WHICH IS ATTAINED AT THE END OF DESIRE"

Before the first sphere, there are three veils of "negative existence", the Ain, Ain Soph and Ain Soph Aur. "Nothing", "Infinity" and "Infinite Light". They are, and they are not; they are before being as we can comprehend it. That which is our source is a concentration of these states of pre-being. The first state of being is the first sphere, Kether, whose color is "Brilliance". When painting the Tree, one usually uses the brightest white that can be found, but it should be "seen" as the brightest imaginable swirling, moving light. Kether means the "Crown" and is placed above the head, so is it just beyond our comprehension.

Kether is called "Primum Mobile", the "first mover", the "first swirlings". It is not manifestation. It is the cause of manifestation, the first idea of being. Kether is what Richard Bach calls "The Is". Before Kether there *is* nothing. Kether is before force, before form, before the idea of force and form.

Imagine you are standing some distance away from a

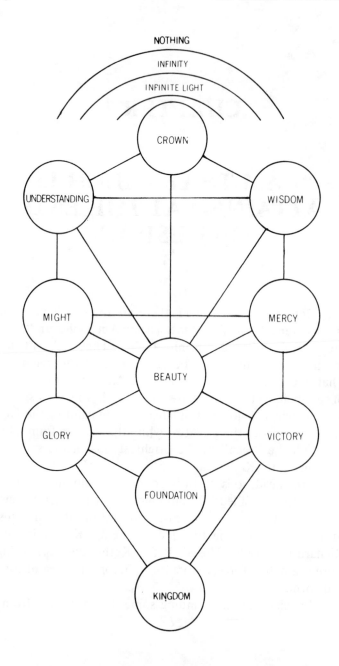

large wall, aiming a flashlight at that wall. At first, the light won't even touch the wall. As you move closer, the tiniest bit of light will reach the wall, so little that it seems a lessening of darkness rather than an addition of light. Move forward slowly. Soon there will be a faint circle of light, and as you move even closer, that circle will become more distinct, smaller, brighter, more concentrated. Eventually you will see a smaller dot of even brighter light in the center of that large circle. That's Kether, coming together out of the Ain Soph, that which is before being. One of Kether's symbols is a point within a circle.

All analogies dealing with the Ultimate must be inadequate, but I offer that one for your consideration and contemplation. We're dealing here with a human mind (mine) and all that can really be given are hints, because that's all I have.

The Deity Name, the Name of Power for this sphere is EHIEH, "I am". This name is another hint toward the understanding of Kether, for it can be compared to a breath. Whisper it to yourself, inhaling on the "Eh" sound and exhaling on "he-yeh". That breath, that exhalation signifies the primal force of Kether becoming the next sphere, Chokmah.

The Archangel of Kether is Metatron, giver of the Qabala. The angels are the "Holy Living Creatures". These are usually depicted as a Man, an Eagle, a Lion and an Ox (Bull). The astrologers among you will recognize these as the symbols for the fixed signs of the Zodiac. The angels symbolized, however, are as far removed from the Zodiac signs as the Zodiac signs are from the physical manifestations.

The Deities usually attributed here are the Creator/ Creatrix Gods and Goddesses: Gaea, Cronos, Ptah, Brahma, etc. Much depends on your own idea of creation. If you believe in a primordial ocean, Kether is that ocean, or the

Cosmic Egg, or the time before the Big Bang, the cause of the Big Bang.

A planetary attribution is difficult. Meditation on the First Swirlings or empty space about to become less empty will be helpful to you.

The Magical Image of Kether is an "ancient bearded ruler seen in profile". Here we encounter another chauvinistic" attribution. We must remember the society that produced the Qabala, one to whom a beard denoted age and wisdom. They combined that age, beard and rulership to represent that which was beyond knowing, the source of all wisdom.

The key phrase here is "seen in profile". The significance of the figure is that only one side is seen; the other is out of sight and will remain so until we rejoin our source, become one with our beginnings.

Kether is androgynous, both male and female, both God and Goddess. Therefore, it would not be inappropriate for pagans to imagine, when using this image, that the side unseen is feminine, the Goddess, for Kether is feminine, receptive to the Ain Soph, and the Unseen Goddess signifies concentration of the not-being of Ain Soph into the idea of being which is Kether.

The spiritual Experience of Kether is "Union with God", or "Reunion with the Source". This is the culmination of the Great Work, the goal for which we all strive, each on our own path, in our own way, aware or unaware. Obviously this is not an experience one has while incarnate. If you did, you wouldn't be.

Kether's Virtue reflects its spiritual experience. It is Attainment, completion of the Great Work. Kether has no Vice.

CHAPTER 4

"I HAVE BEEN WITH THEE FROM THE BEGINNING"

As many Qabalistic texts say, "Kether overflows into the next sphere," Chokmah, whose name means "Wisdom". Pure being becomes pure force — not physical force, we are still a long way from physical manifestation. Chokmah is the *idea* of force, spiritual force. Chokmah is the Ultimate Positive, the God.

This sphere and those directly below it are said to be on the Masculine Pillar, and Chokmah sits at its head. Chokmah is the Great Stimulator, dynamic thrust, the Great Fertilizer. Its name of Power is JHVH, Yahveh or Yah, meaning "Lord". I sometimes translate this "Father of all".

Many sources use the name "Jehovah" for JHVH but this is incorrect. Ancient Hebrew, when written, recorded only consonants. In Judaism, the word represented by JHVH is not spoken except in prayer and in a worship service. The word "Adonai" is spoken whenever the letters JHVH are written. In the twelfth century, a copyist was

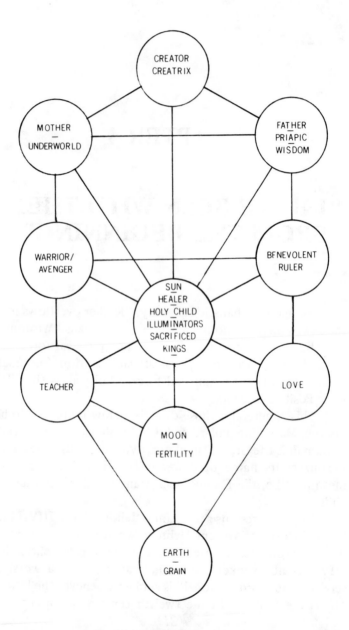

DEITIES

apparently translating Hebrew script into the Roman alphabet, and was confused by the vowels for "Adonai" written under the JHVH, as a reminder to the reader to say "Adonai". Thus appeared "Jehovah". The proper word is "Yahveh" or "Yah".

Deity names are usually vibrated in use, that is, pronounced resonantly, almost chanted, syllable by syllable, in a tone you can feel physically in your body. This vibration usually occurs in your throat and chest. Real experts can direct the vibration to any part of the body.

JHVH when used is usually vibrated as it is spelled in Hebrew; "Yod heh vav he". There's a tendency to pronounce the "vav" as "Vo", probably because it rhymes with "Yod". Pronounce this aloud, and you get something very similar to the traditional pagan salute, "IO EVOHE".

Ratzkiel is the archangel of Chokmah. The angels which carry out Ratzkiel's directions are the Auphanim, the Wheels, a name full of symbolism. The Wheel of Life. The invention of the wheel represents one of man's first uses *of* natural forces (gravity, inertia) instead of fighting against them.

In the Old Testament, Ezekiel saw among other things, "wheels" in a vision. Isn't it possible that what he saw was not a wheel as we know it, (nor a space ship, for that matter), but a choir of "auphanim", and that the special meaning was lost in translation? In support of this theory is the fact that Ezekiel also saw "Living Creatures" who bore the likeness of an eagle, an ox, a lion and a man. Put the word "holy" in front of "living creatures" and you have the angelic army of Kether. A few lines later, Ezekiel refers to the "likeness of a throne". "Thrones" are the angels of Binah, the next sphere.

The Spiritual Experience of this sphere is the "Vision of God Face to Face" or "Vision of the Source we Seek". This is another experience that is not usually had while

one is incarnate. Chokmah represents pure force, and as
such, total formlessness. If one identified with total formlessness, totally, one could not remain in a form. Considering the spiritual advancement necessary to reach and identify
with this sphere, it is unlikely one would be able to have
this experience while in a body. Most of mankind can barely
look themselves squarely in the face — much less face the
Ultimate.

There may be exceptions. Biblical stories of "ascen-
sions" could be such occurrences.

The Deities found in Chokmah are of three types, each
reflecting a facet of this sphere. All Great Father Gods go
here: Odin, the Dagda, Olorun, Zeus/Jupiter (especially
Jupiter who seems to have fathered half the population of
the Mediterranean). Dius Pitar (say that ten times very
quickly) would belong here as would the father aspect of
Yahveh.

The Priapic Gods are attributed to this sephira, for
Chokmah represents the absolute in the ability to fertilize;
fertility in its most abstract, far from the physical. One of
the symbols for Chokmah is the penis, long venerated in
ancient cultures as a symbol of the dynamic life force.
This is the Great God Pan, not Pan the satyr, although this
does not imply that physical sex and fertility are less holy
than this spiritual fertility. We simply have not reached the
physical yet.

The ancient truth "That which is above is as that
which is below, but after another manner" certainly applies
here. Physical fertility is a reflection, a more physically
concrete one, of the fertility of Chokmah, just as the union
of man and woman is a joining of the Lord and Lady. Neither is more holy — they are simply manifestations of the
same thing on a different plane.

Because Chokmah is called "Wisdom" one can attribute
Pallas Athene here as well as Isis-Urania, Vishnu, Kwan

Shi Yin.

The Magical Image of Chokmah is a bearded male figure — the Father, Jung's Archetypal Old Man.

The Virtue is Devotion. Having seen your Source, what else could you feel, what else be filled with?

Chokmah is half of the first two pairs on the Tree of Life. The Pairs must always be considered together, in relation to each other, for it is impossible to understand one without the other.

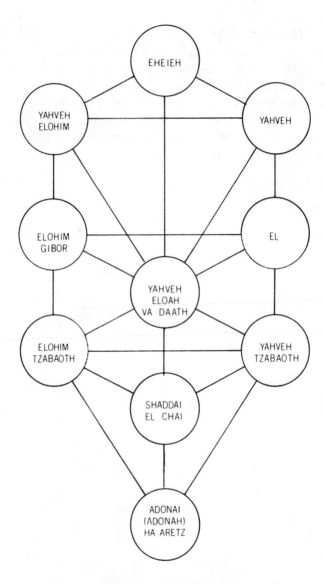

NAMES   OF POWER

CHAPTER 5

"LISTEN TO THE WORDS OF THE GREAT MOTHER"

Many books of the Mystical Qabala say that each of the spheres emanates from the one before. Pagans may have a problem with this because Binah is the sphere of the Goddess, and they are not going to like the implication of the Goddess emanating from the God. Other sources say that all spheres emanated from the Ain Soph at the same time, they are all one, all part of each other. Remember that even this wonderful gift to mankind is an abstraction, man struggling to express the inexpressible, and a poor representation of what truly is, especially at this level.

Binah is the sphere whose name means "Understanding" or "Intelligence". Use your intelligence and understanding so that you won't miss the marvels of the Qabala by objecting to the way it is phrased.

Binah represents negativity, receptivity, passivity. It is form, force in pattern. Its color is black, a color in which all light rays are absorbed and none reflected. Without black, the absence of reflected light rays, there are no visual patterns. Without Binah, there are no forms.

The Planetary Attribution of Binah is Saturn, known as the "Restrictor", and form *is* restriction, a very necessary one. Steam with no restriction accomplishes nothing; restricted, it can power an engine. When we cast a magic circle, part of its purpose is to create a limited area in which to work, to concentrate our energies within the restriction of the circle rather than try to control the energies of the entire room.

Binah is also resistance, a springboard. If you've ever tried to push anything through water that was over your head, you'll appreciate the value of resistance. Those of you with a military bent can compare Binah to the thrust block so necessary to the workings of the big cannons.

On a less impersonal level, Binah is the Goddess, the Great Mother, the Womb of Life, the Cauldron of Cerridwen. She sits at the Head of the Feminine Pillar, the Pillar of Form, of Restriction.

All Great Mother Goddesses are in Binah, obviously; Isis, Danu, Demeter, Yemanja, Frigga — and Goddesses which represent the Feminine Aspect: Sakti, Maya, Kwan Yin. Because of the Saturn aspect, Bran is placed here, although he goes equally well in others.

For several reasons, I would place the God/desses of the Underworld in this sphere. The "dead" are also the unborn, and therefore the Womb of Life would not only be the place of the beginning of life, but its end. At the end of an incarnation, we return to Binah, divested on the way through Geburah of those things to be left behind, are broken down and after a time, reborn. It seems only logical that the sphere of form, the first supernal inkling of form would equate to that.

The spiritual Experience of this sephira is the "Vision of Sorrow". This is the kind of sorrow most of us are not likely to experience, simply because we could not bear it.

This is Isis, searching for the pieces of her mutilated husband, Mary at the foot of the Cross, Branwen, betrayed and enslaved by her husband, Demeter weeping for Persephone. This vision is, perhaps, seeing through the eyes of the Goddess — seeing what we must struggle through to grow. It is the pain the Lady feels when we weep.

Binah's Angels are the Aralim, the Thrones. One alternate title for Binah is Khorsia, the Throne. Isis means "throne" and her symbol in hieroglyphs is a throne.

Although most of us will not experience the Vision of Sorrow completely in this lifetime, no life is without its sorrows, its trials. Sorrow is, unfortunately, one of the best teachers, and we learn most through our difficult times. It is said that we are never given any trial without being given strength to bear it, and the Aralim are the source of that strength. A throne, on the physical plane, is a large, often massive chair — sturdy and stable. It is usually mounted on an even sturdier platform. You can imagine yourself curled up in a huge chair, surrounded by it, feeling its stability and strength; you are held safe, though the very world is shaken.

Over them all is Tzafkiel, the Archangel of Binah. He is the Keeper of the Akashic Records, where all the days of our lives are recorded, the lessons we've learned, and those we have yet to learn.

He is also the Archangel of the Archetypal Temple. I always have this vision of an open-air temple in the clouds, and all the prayers and sounds of worship of all the people of all religions of all time reach this beautiful place in the form of music, each belief a diffferent note, all blending and harmonizing into a mighty and incredibly lovely melody, ever changing and ever glorious. I can almost hear it. Listen!

Tzafkiel cares for this temple, guards it, and guides all sincere religious fellowships.

I had an experience while writing this chapter that might demonstrate how potent the correspondences of the Qabala can be.

"The Vision of Sorrow" brought to mind a quote from *The Prophet*: "The deeper sorrow carves into your being, the more joy you can contain". I remembered a line from the televsion show *Kung Fu*. "I seek only to be a cup, empty of myself, filled with Oneness". Cup . . . chalice . . . cauldron . . . water . . . sea . . . the great seas of the world . . . source of life . . . womb of life . . . Binah. I looked back at my notes and saw that another name for Binah is "Marah, the Great Sea".

The Magical Image of Binah is a Matron, a Mature Woman, the Goddess as Mother and/or Crone. Both are appropriate. Two of Binah's titles are "Ama", the dark, sterile Mother, and "Aima", the bright fertile mother. Aima gives us birth on our descent to physical matter, incarnation. Ama receives us as we return to suffer the greater death of Self, striving ever toward oneness.

In these two names, by the way, we find an example of Temura. "Ama" becomes "Aima" with the addition of the letter "yod" which is itself a symbol of fertility.

The Name of Power is "Yahveh Elohim", usually translated as the "Lord God", which is not only inappropriate, but inaccurate. "Elohim" comes from "Eloah" which is a feminine word, and "Him" which is a masculine plural ending. A more accurate translation would be "Goddess/Gods". Concentrate on the sounds, knowing that it signifies the Goddess. You won't be wrong. You know what the sphere represents . . . vibrate "Yahveh Elohim" and think "Mother", and all will be well.

Binah's Vice is Avarice, Greed — a very negative aspect of receptivity and in-gathering, clutching all you gather to you.

Sybil Leek, when asked the difference between meditation and prayer, answered that prayer was talking to the gods; meditation was listening to them. Binah is very much involved with meditation, for its Virtue is Silence. When you are talking, you are not listening. Silence is being receptive, allowing the inward flow to enter freely.

The following exercise is an unusual form of meditation on this Virtue. It is not easy to do, but you will find the effects very interesting.

This exercise requires the cooperation of a friend or two, and it will not work if not done in the presence of others. The practice of the exercise is simply this: Do not speak for at least four, and preferably six to eight hours.

The first hour or two will be difficult. You'll be bursting with ideas, answers, comments. Be still. Eventually you'll see results. Because you are not going to make a response to what is being said, you will listen closely instead of listening with part of your mind and formulating a response with the other. You will listen in a way you've never experienced, hear more than before, understand the value of silence. You will also find it relaxing, because you are freed from the responsibility of responding. Nothing is expected of you.

Chokmah and Binah are that which is represented by the Tai Chi'n symbol, the Yin and the Yang. They are primal force and primal form, the ideas of force and form, masculine and feminine, active and passive, positive and negative. Between these two spheres, the Great Father and the Great Mother, is spun the web of life. They are the ebb and the flow, the coming and going, the gathering-in and the going-out. They are of no consequence without the other, for nothing can be built, or even be, without force *and* form.

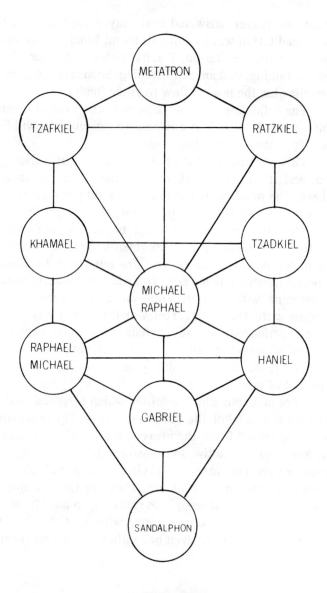

ARCHANGELS

CHAPTER 6

"THERE SHALL YE ASSEMBLE"

The Three Spheres we have discussed so far are called "The Supernal Triangle", and they represent potential. Chesed, the second sphere on the Pillar of Force is the first sphere to represent actuality. Its name means "Mercy" or "Grace" and it is also known as "Gedulah", "Greatness".

Here we find the benevolent ruler gods: Zeus/Jupiter, Indra, Amoun, Osiris. As you can see already, a Deity can easily fit into more than one sphere. As you continue to read, you will find yourself placing others.

Chesed's Planetary Attribution is Jupiter, the Expander. In astrology, Jupiter is referred to as a benefic planet, unlike Saturn, which precedes it, and Mars, which follows it. Times are changing, but modern day society seems to call that which is easy and peaceful "benefic" and that which is difficult and requires some effort, "Malefic". We pagans have learned, however, that difficulties are lessons, opportunities for growth, and if they cannot honestly be greeted with cries of joy, they can at least be accepted and understood.

Difficulties, however, are more appropriately discussed in the next chapter. Chesed is a sphere that *can* provide help for those difficulties. It is called the "Hall of the Masters", the "Sphere of the Adepts". It is in Chesed, according to tradition, that those souls who have reached a certain stage in their development stop, by choice, and remain here in order to be of help to those of us still struggling toward growth. These souls are often referred to as the Ascended Masters. In the Craft, we call them the Ancient Ones.

The Magical Image of Chesed is "A wise and kindly king upon a throne". This king is the father of his people, building industry, fostering learning, patronizing the arts. His kingdom is at peace. He is nuturing expansion and order. Osiris, for example, taught his people the way of agriculture, organized growing, a more stable form of life than the nomadic. Chesed is the sphere of order, the first cohesion of force affected by form, on a very subtle archetypal level.

Chesed's Spiritual Experience is the "Vision of Love"; indeed, "Love" is often used as an alternate name for this sphere. The Experience can be called the "Understanding of Perfect Love". Chesed emanates from Binah, Understanding, and the two are inseparable; there cannot be love without understanding, and true understanding must bring love. This is love without judgment, without assessment, love of that which is within all creation, of that which we share, each of us, love of and from the God and Goddess. It is a total recognition of the God/dess within ourselves and others, recognition of our oneness. It is the ability to see past all the layers we humans cover ourselves with, for Chesed is beyond human, beyond incarnation.

In certain magical lodges, the grade given to one who has reached Chesed in that long climb back of the Tree is "Adeptus Exemptus", one who is exempt from the Wheel of Life, of physical incarnation. Surely one who has reached this level, one who is so close to that from which we all come is capable of a forgiveness, an understanding that is Perfect Love.

It is highly improbable that the grade "Adeptus Exemptus" would be given to one who was still incarnate, but not impossible. However, I've met many people who "confided" to me that this was their "last life", and none of them had the qualities that one would expect in such an advanced soul.

The Virtue of this sphere is Obedience, but not the blind obedience of a slave. No proper teacher of the Western esoteric traditions would teach students to obey without question, without thought. A true teacher prepares the student for independence, for the use of the mind and logic processes. The student's spiritual advancement is her or his own responsibility, after all, and no teacher can make that advancement for a student. One large difference between Craft and Christianity is that we have no one "saving" us. All we accomplish must be through our own efforts, although we are helped from time to time, and help others when we are able. (We don't have any devil to blame our failures on, either!)

We must bring about our own advancement. Yet, as that growth occurs, students may find themselves doing exactly what the teacher wished, but because the student has decided it is the proper thing to do, not because the teacher wished it. "Obedience" at Chesed is having your own will so aligned with that of the God/dess that it is impossible for your to do other than they wish, because your wish is the same as theirs. This is not forced agreement, forced obedience. When Chesed is reached in spiritual growth, the Will *will* be that of the Lord and Lady, because it is right.

The Vice is any of those corruptions of power, of

those in power, bigotry, hyprocrisy, gluttony, tyranny.

The Name of Power is "El", God.

The Chasmalim, the Brilliant ones, are Chesed's angels and they are led by Tzadkiel, Archangel of Chesed. This archangel and angels are especially helpful to those suffering from instability of any kind; spiritual, mental or emotional.

This animal which represents Chesed is the unicorn. Concentration on a symbol of a sphere can bring contact with that sphere, and the upsurge in the popularity of the unicorn could be an unconscious (and in many cases, conscious) invocation of the powers of Chesed. This is noteworthy in present times when world events are so definitely more indicative of Geburah, the next sphere, than they are of Chesed. Chesedic influences are usually pleasant, easy to take, and Geburah is not so pleasant.

CHAPTER 7

"AND YE SHALL BE FREE"

The Sephira Geburah, "Might", is also known as Din, "Judgment", and Pachad, "Fear", all of which seem to bode ill for any dealings with this sphere. The actions of Geburah *can* be difficult, but it is not a "malefic" sphere.

Paganfolk have a better understanding of the actions of this sphere than many others in the modern world. An "easy life" with no hardships, no trials, all wishes fulfilled, and so forth, would be a sign of blessing to many. We pagans would consider it restful, but such a life seldom contributes anything to total growth. As I mentioned in the previous chapter, we might not give joyful welcome to the trials and tribulations of life, but we can accept them for the lesson they contain, the growth they make possible.

One of the things I lost (without regret) when I came to the Craft was that heart-rending cry into the darkness, "Why?" There was usually no answer, not even an echo. I might not receive an answer even now, but I no longer cry into the darkness. I *know* there is a reason, and that I

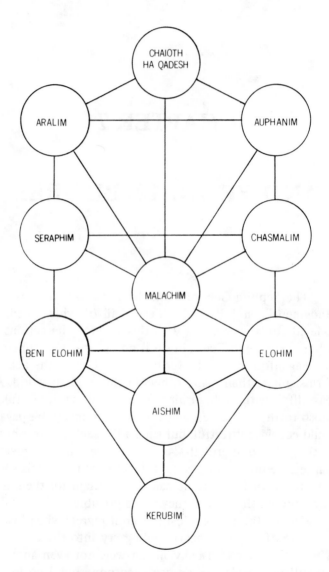

ANGELS (Hebrew)

will eventually understand. I am not afraid of the influences of Geburah. They are an integral part of the workings of the Goddess, and as necessary to all existence as Chesed.

The "fear" reflected in the title "Pachad" would be better translated as "awe", especially awe of natural forces. It is the feeling you get watching films of Mt. St. Helen as it erupts, or see "before and after" pictures.

It is also the wonderful feeling depicted in the lovely scene from Kenneth Grahame's *Wind in the Willows*, when Rat and Mole find themselves in the presence of Pan:

> All this he saw, for one moment breathless and intense, vivid on the morning sky; and still, as he looked, he lived; and still as he lived, he wondered.
>
> "Rat!" he found breath to whisper, shaking. "Are you afraid?"
>
> "Afraid?" murmured the Rat, his eyes shining with unutterable love. "Afraid of *Him*? O, never, never! And yet—and yet—O, Mole, I am afraid!"

The term "God-fearing" should mean this, not abject terror of a power that will strike you with a lightning bolt at the slightest transgression.

Geburah's planetary attribution is, of course, Mars, and Geburah, like Mars is so easily misunderstood. It represents destruction, the breaking down of form.

The Magical Image of this sphere is a "mighty warrior in his chariot (or her chariot if you prefer; a warrior queen is an acceptable and possibly more ancient image). While the benevolent king in Chesed rules and nurtures, the warrior king of Geburah defends and punishes. Many ancient kings were in front of their soldiers as they charged into battle.

Statues of Egyptian Pharoahs held a crook and a flail; the crook to guide their people and the flail to punish transgressors. These statues reflect an understanding of the need for balance between Chesed and Geburah in the rhythm of life.

White blood cells perform Geburic function in your

body, your inner kingdom. The surgeon who removes a cancer or lances an abscess does the same.

Consider the Grand Canyon, result of millions of years of wearing down, of destruction of form, and tell me that such a glorious thing is the result of something malefic.

Another less obvious but equally valid example is the London Fire. The destruction of life and property is awful to contemplate, but remember, the Fire occurred at the height of the plague. Rats bearing the disease-carrying fleas were abundant in the slums, most of which were destroyed by the fire, wiping out the source of the plague. Without this destruction, the whole of Europe might have been devastated, not to mention what could have happened to the population of England.

The rhythm on which we place so much emphasis in the Craft is an integral part of the workings of the Qabala, as seen by the strong emphasis on the ebb and flow of energies between the three pairs of spheres. Geburah's place in the scheme of things is foolish to ignore, because we live with it every day.

We are dealing with Geburah every time we eat. Our food is broken down, releasing energy for our bodies. The form of the food is sacrificed to release the life force we must have to live. Yes, *sacrificed*, for sacrifice is nothing more than the destruction of form to release force.

We do this every time we burn a candle, start the car, turn up the heater. In ancient times of blood sacrifice, the body was destroyed to release the life force within. We no longer make blood sacrifices (except at the Blood Bank), but we are still involved with the forces of Geburah every moment we live, and after.

At this point in our discussion of the Universal Tree, let us consider the earthly tree. It grows in its proper season, and in the Autumn the leaves change color and die, falling to the ground. There, in the natural course of events, they would break down, become part of the earth, and nourish the very tree that produced them. This is Nature's way. The tree becomes large and stronger in its Chesed cycle *because* of its Geburah cycle.

This is, of course, unless some fool has carted the leaves away and burned them, thereby not only depriving the tree of its rightful nourishment, but polluting the air as well. This idiot pays for his stupidity by ending up with a starving tree, or spending a fortune on chemical fertilizers to replace that which Mother Nature would have provided herself, left alone. If a garden *must* be neat, let us hope the gathered leaves were placed in a compost heap which not only allows, but encourages the Geburah of Nature to work. Organic gardeners understand Geburah.

Why is the rest of the world so afraid of it that they even deny its existence? Our bodily secretions and excretions rid our bodies of things which are useless and/or dangerous. The ancient Romans even had a Goddess who ruled over the natural excretions of the body, knowing as they did that this function is as holy as any other.

Our very laws reflect this fear. All during our lives, we eat food which has drawn its nourishment directly or indirectly from the Earth. When we die, do we put our bodies into the ground so that the Geburic cycle can take place? Nope. We embalm them, saving them for I don't know what, and depriving the Earth of the minerals which are rightly hers to claim.

All the energies represented by the Tree will function as they must. If blocked, they will try to burst through the blockage. With the energies of Geburah, this could result in a war, or some natural disaster . . . or several! Noticed a plethora of natural disasters lately, hmmmm?

While the War gods such as Mars and Ares are obvious attributions to Geburah, you can also place Minerva/Athena who would become a warrior in defense of those who have been wronged, as you could attribute Bran, when he avenged the wrong done his sister. Kali represents the destructive force.

I place the "Smith" gods here: Tubal, Cain, Vulcan/Hephaestus—to reflect another aspect of Geburah. This sphere is called the "Hall of Karma", the "Hall of Judgement". As the smith pounds his creation into shape, plunges it again and again into the fire, bends and shapes and purifies it until he has a strong, perfect weapon or tool, so does the process of Karma perfect our spirits with the energies of Geburah. It never destroys that which is eternal, never the essence, but only that which is unnecessary and temporary. When we rid ourselves of unnecessary weight, we've lost nothing necessary to us, no part of our true selves. We've been freed from a burden we were carrying around unnecessarily. Breaking any bad habit frees us from its control.

Geburah's virtues are Energy and Courage, both fairly obvious in view of the meaning of the sphere. The Vices are Cruelty and *Wanton* Destruction.

Imagine that you stand before a giant glacier. With a snap of your fingers, you can cause that glacier to crumble into billions of ice cubes.

Imagine that you stand on the world's highest mountain. With a whisper, you can create a hundred mile per hour wind that has the power to sweep all the way around the world.

Imagine that you can, with the blink of an eyelash, destroy this planet. Imagine if you can, controlling this kind of power. Take a few minutes.

Can you get a glimpse of that power? This is the merest hint of one aspect of the Spritual Experience of Geburah, the "Vision of Power".

Now returning to the capabilities mentioned above, remember this. When that glacier crumbles, it is going to fill that lake in front of it and send a giant wave right over the place where you are standing.

That 100 m.p.h. wind is going to circle the globe, destroying everything in its path, carry with it a good deal of debris (trees, people, cars, building), come up behind you and remove you from that mountain with considerable force.

If you destroy the planet you are standing on . . .

The Vision of Power is a realization of the power which you can control *and* a realization of the results of and responsibility for the use of that power. This *is* the Hall of Karma, and never is the understanding of cause and effect so great as in this experience.

The Name of Power is Elohim Gibor, "Almighty Gods and Goddessess", or "Almighty Ones".

Several weapons and such are symbols of Geburah, but the most interesting is that all five-sided figures are symbolic of this sphere, including the pentagon. Is it coincidence, I wonder, that our national armed forces have their headquarters in a five-sided building called the "Pentagon"?

Geburah's archangel is the mighty Khamael, protector of the weak, avenger of the wronged. He leads the Seraphim, the Fiery Serpents (much like the Greek Furies) in the performance of their duties—the slaying of dragons, defense of the inner country—King Arthur's "might *for* right".

In the Golden Dawn ritual for the initiation of the Neophyte, we are told "Unbalanced mercy is weakness and the fading away of the will. Unbalanced Severity is cruelty and barrenness of mind". Again, we come to the consideration of two opposites on the tree, this time Geburah and Chesed. If it seems to you that these sephiroth are on the wrong pillars, consider this: Chesed expands, Geburah restricts.

" . . . *let there be power and compassion* . . ."

My husband and I are involved in an activity indicative of the balancing of Geburah and Chesedic energies: an exercise program. We are using exercises to burn off calories and free ourselves from excess pounds put there by a little Chesedic gluttony, using energy to make ourselves healthy and therefore creating *more* energy. It takes courage to tell those aching muscles to move and will power to get in there and do it. We are breaking down form (fat) to release force (body heat and energy).

There will be a further balance eventually; this activity is not entirely Geburic and shouldn't be. Those muscles, screaming right now, will be built into strong healthy muscles. Some of that flab will be replaced by firm flesh. Geburah and Chesed will work together, balanced as they should be.

Chesed's idealism is balanced by the realism of Geburah. They are the latent and kinetic energies of the universe, the building up of power and the ebbing away, anabolism and catabolism, the waxing and waning moon.

Always consider one with the other, and you will understand both much better.

CHAPTER 8

LET THERE BE BEAUTY

We have reached the center of the Tree, its heart, its pivot point, the sphere whose name means Beauty or Harmony, Tifareth. It is equilibrium, the epitome of balance. Tifareth *is* the balance between Mercy and Severity, between active and passive, force and form. It is the child of the God and Goddess.

Its Planetary attribution is the Sun, center of our solar system. All planets move around the Sun in their various orbits, as the spheres are placed around Tifareth. Interesting, is it not, that the sphere which, as you will see, would be suitable for no other celestial attribution *but* the Sun, should be placed in the center of the Tree at a time when the Sun was not considered the center of the Universe?

Esoteric tradition holds that the power of our Sun comes from another "Sun". So does the power of Tifareth, called the "Lesser Countenance", reflect the power of the "Greater Countenance", Kether.

Tifareth's Pagan Mythology is multitudinous, because

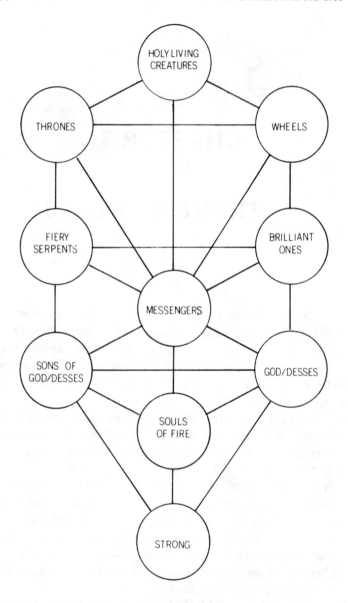

ANGELS (English)

Tifareth has two aspects, Death and Re-birth.

In this sphere are placed the Sacrificed Kings: Osiris, Llew, Dionysius, Adonis, Balder. Also placed here are the Sacred Children: Horus, Jesus, Gwern, Lugh and others.

Because of the solar attribution of Tifareth, the Sun symbolic of Life, Light, Healing and Illumination, you find healing gods, Sun Deities (Ra, Apollo, Rama, Amaterasu) *and* the Givers of Illumination: Krishna, Buddha, Mithra and others.

Another Tifareth figure in mythology, although not a deity, is King Arthur. According to legend, Arthur advocated the use of force for protection of those who needed it — might *for* right — instead of might is right. That *idea* is Geburic, but the advancement in ideas, the illumination, is an aspect of Tifareth. The bringers of illumination are not necessarily religious figures. They are those who attempt to teach us better ways to do things and try to help humanity better its lot. Osiris is revered not only as a god, but as a man who taught his people agriculture. Ghandi was a man, not a god, but very definitely offered a new way of thinking, and Dr. Martin Luther King carried on his tradition. Each of us will have others in mind that have Tifareth qualities. The ones I've mentioned have one other thing in common. They were murdered. They often are.

There are two Spiritual Experiences of Tifareth, just as there are two aspects. The first is "The Vision of the Harmony of Things", the knowledge that the "Universe is unfolding as it should". It is the Tao. One who has truly experienced this is often removed from ordinary irritations and worries, because they have seen the Harmony, the Big Picture, and they understand there is a reason for all.

When you begin to look at things from a Qabalistic point of view, you'll ponder the advancement of people, wonder which experiences they've had, where they would be on the Tree. In modern history, I believe that Ghandi had seen the Vision of the Harmony of Things, or come close. His priorities seem to reflect that. How a person worshipped was not important. Self-respect was, and understanding was, but status was not. Ghandi-ji was not a saint —I'm told he was a rotten father— but he taught another way of thinking, a more mature way, and one that exhibited a rare kind of courage.

Jesus of Nazareth is probably the most modern of the sacrificed kings. The Adeptus Minor Ritual, the Tifareth initiation in magical lodges, was a ritual death and burial (simulated of course). We are all familiar with his death . . . an Adeptus Minor ritual that was not a simulation. For those of us who have become Craft after being raised Christian, he remains a great teacher who taught many things we can easily agree with.

Ghandi may have had the second Spiritual Experience, and certainly Jesus did. I express this as "Understanding the Mysteries of Sacrifice". It is usually called the "Understanding of the Mysteries of the Crucifixion", but crucifixion is only one form of sacrifice, and contemplation on all the sacrificed kings, whatever their manner of death, should bring results.

Pagans of all traditions are accused of barbaric blood sacrifices, and the accusations were true at one time. True, not only of nature religions, but of Judaism and Christianity. What modern folk do not understand is the attitude of the Sun King, the meaning of his sacrifice. Believing as they did that the present life was only one of many, these kings did not fear death of the body. They offered that body, the life force it contained, and the Personality they possessed at that time, as a gift to the Gods and to their people, believing that this sacrifice advanced them spiritually. Their next life would be better, and the present life of the people they represented would be better. This presents a far different picture than the unwilling sacrifice, screaming and cursing. The energy would be released, it is true, but not the kind of energy that would be beneficial.

There are three Magical Images for Tifareth: A king, a child, and a sacrificed god. The one chosen would depend on the aspect of Tifareth you wish to contact.

In my tradition, as in others, both second and third degree initiations relate to Tifareth. Second degree represents the ritual death; the initiate dies to an old life and is re-born to a life of service to the Goddess and her Lord. Then comes a time of spiritual testing. When this period is over, the Third Degree takes place, to celebrate the re-birth of the High Priest or High Priestess.

Authorities will give one or two archangels for Tifareth, Michael or Raphael. Raphael is appropriate because he is the Archangel of Air, and Tifareth is on the Middle Pillar, the Air Pillar. He is also the Healing Archangel, and Tifareth is the sphere of healing.

Tifareth is also the sphere of the Sun, and Michael is the Archangel of Fire, having some healing aspects as well.

Once again, our filing cabinet analogy comes to our rescue. The Archangel you work with is the one most applicable to the work you are doing. There is ample room in our drawer for more than one archangel file folder.

Yahveh Eloah Va Daath, "God/dess made manifest in the sphere of the mind" is the Name of Power for Tifareth.

Its Virtue is "Devotion to the Great Work", dedication to the deliberate evolution of your soul. The Vice is Pride. Do not confuse pride with self-respect in this instance. It would be better expressed as "False Pride", or "Lack of Humility".

We are all part of the Lord and Lady; they are within us. To consider ourselves unworthy of respect would be to dishonor Them within us. However, they are within *all* of us, and having worked to achieve Tifareth consciousness does not make you a better person than anyone else. Humility can be expressed, "I am no more and no less than you". To have humility does not mean to be a doormat, it means recognition of the equality of the God and Goddess within, and within others. Those who have not reached Tifareth are not lesser, any more than are children who are physically younger.

One animal attributed to Tifareth expresses much of what the sphere represents. It is the Phoenix, which dies in flame and is reborn from its ashes, again and again.

CHAPTER 9

"FOR BEHOLD, ALL ACTS OF LOVE AND PLEASURE ARE MY RITUALS"

We return to the Pillar of Force to Netzach, "Victory"; Victory in the sense of Achievement. In my coven, which uses the Tree of Life as a framework for development, it is after work with Netzach that a student reaches First Degree. This requires so much work and time that it *is* quite an achievement.

Netzach is emotion, love in all forms. Its Pagan Mythology includes Venus, Aphrodite, Hathor and Rhiannon. Its Planetary Attribution is, naturally, Venus. This makes Netzach seemingly easy to understand, but not necessarily so.

The Archangel is Haniel, who is a patron of the arts. His angels are the Elohim. As you've learned, this word can be translated as "Goddesses/Gods". How can Gods and Goddesses be angels? They are not, of course. What is represented here is the energy of the image we have given each deity in our minds. It is in Netzach that the pure Deity energy is actually broken into the various aspects of the

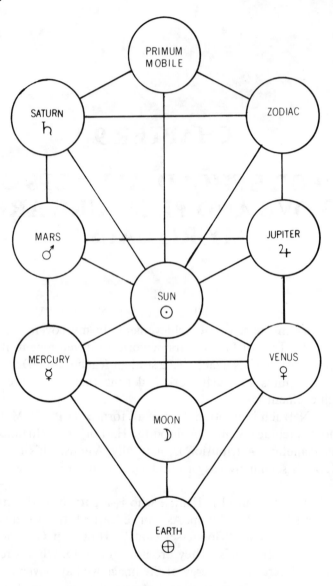

PLANETARY   ATTRIBUTIONS

Lord and Lady we are familiar with, the *energy* not the forms—they come later. Netzach is like a prism which divides light into rainbow colors.

Netzach's Spiritual Experience is the "Vision of Beauty Triumphant". All of us have touched this experience when, in a moment of great, almost unbearable beauty, we have glimpsed infinity. Having known such a moment, this experience is a knowledge that the Harmony, the Beauty of Tifareth will triumph. If you have touched such a moment, briefly, imagine the glory of a complete Spiritual Experience in this sphere.

The Name of Power is "Yahveh Tzabaoth". Never mind how it translates. What it means is the *opposite* of "E Pluribus Unum". It means "out of the one, many", all the facets of the God and Goddess as we have seen them in all their glorious ways.

We have here a sphere at the base of the Masculine Pillar, and it is chock full of Goddesses. How so? This is one of the reasons I prefer to call this the Pillar of Force. Netzach is energy, creative energy, the energy you put into rituals to make them effective. The form of the rituals themselves come under Hod, the next sphere.

This sphere is the spark of genius that touches us when we are being creative. It is the energy you feel when you are writing a ritual; the energy that turns it into a "given" ritual instead of a written one.

In the *White Goddess*, Robert Graves spends 500 pages discussing the fact that no poet deserves the name unless his poetry is directed to and inspired by the Goddess. (Imagine, 500 pages about Netzach) Graves says that the "muse" that real poets and artists credit with inspiration for their work is none other than the Triple Goddess. (We hear of nine muses now, but Mr. Graves says there is only one. She was "divided" by some patriarchal chauvinist in a "divide and conquer" move.)

Netzach represents that spark which makes the difference between a craftsman and an artist, between a rhyme and a poem.

The Virtue of Netzach is Unselfishness. Naturally, love, true love, would be unselfish. The Vice is Unchastity. This is not an attempt to impose upon you the ethics of another religion. Unchastity, or Impurity do not necessarily relate to your sex life. Motives can be impure, too.

A psychologist of my acquaintance deals (unbeknownst to her) almost entirely with Netzach energy with her patients. Although the majority of her clients are artists and writers, those who are *not* benefit from "art therapy" as well.

My psychologist friend has learned the value of positive Netzach energies—not the aspect of emotion, which, when untempered by the logic and reason of the next sphere can result in a person totally ruled by emotion, but by the *creative energy* of Netzach.

In her therapy, she encourages her patients to create, especially in the visual arts (painting, sculpture, etc.). The *quality* of the artwork is unimportant to the therapy; the importance is in the act of creation.

We have much better contacts with Netzach when we are children, because we are freely creative. We paint, write stories and poems, and model clay only for the joy of creating. There comes a time, however, when we become concerned with the quality of our creativity, rather than the fun of creation. We worry about whether our paintings or poems are "good" or not. If they are not, we stop creating them, and cut ourselves off from the Netzach energy.

If you would develop Netzach contacts, get out your paints and paint a picture just for the fun of it. It doesn't matter a jot whether it is "good". Throw it away if you like. Write horrible poems, or the world's worst short story. While you are being creative, you are touching and being touched by the Netzach energies and that is infinitely more important than the results that appear on paper.

We will learn more about Netzach if we study Hod.

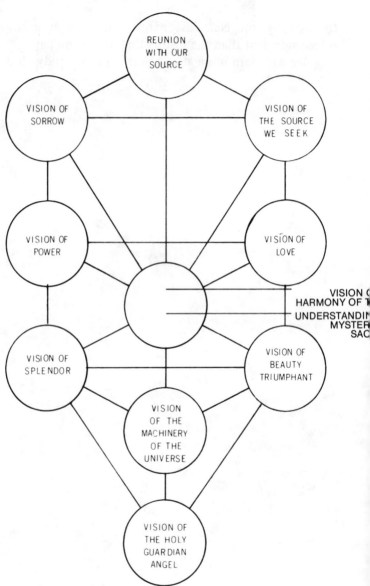

SPIRITUAL EXPERIENCES

CHAPTER 10

"TO THESE SHALL I TEACH THAT WHICH IS AS YET UNKNOWN"

Hod means "Glory", or "Splendor" and is the sphere of the intellect. Hod represents science and teaching, and all teaching gods and messengers are attributed to this sphere. All intellectual activities of the mind are here: books, communications, esoteric teachings, the text of rituals, puns, puzzles and cryptograms.

Hod's Planetary Attribution is Mercury, the planet which receives the most light from the Sun.

The Vice of Hod is Falsehood, Dishonesty. This may or may not be a deliberate falsehood; it may be dishonesty with self. When the energy of Hod begins to have an effect, one develops a tremendous talent for rationalization. Their logic, if it is not based on truth, will not be truth, but it will be wonderfully logical. Work with and in Hod can stimulate the intellect and its processes, and unfortunately, these can be used to rationalize decisions with great wit and cunning, whether or not these ideas are based on truth and right.

I have seen this self-deception manifest in a very interesting and very "Hodic" way; the student might believe that form is all—that if he or she does a right in the right way at the right time and with the precise words, exact pronunciation, one doesn't have to worry about handling energies, developing will. There is no need to use self-discipline, take care of one's mind. The edict against the use of "recreational" drugs is ridiculous. (This edict exists in my group.) The student can also get very hung-up on books, etc. Only that which is printed is valid. Even typed words do not get the respect printed words do, and verbal teachings are totally discounted.

The Virtue is Truthfulness. Oh, what a difficult virtue it can be to achieve, what a painful one! It involves not only truth with others, but must include truthfulness with self, that most difficult, most agonizing truth to bear.

The onset of this Virtue can be as disconcerting as any Vice. Some interpret "being totally honest" as "letting it all hang out", and "saying what I really feel, man". For some reason, what they "really feel" is all negative. It takes some time to realize that this truthfulness should include the positive things that are felt, and that truthfulness need not be tactless and inconsiderate.

There are two archangels attributed to Hod: Raphael and Michael. Hod is situated directly below Geburah, home of Khamael, defender of the wronged and protector of the weak. Michael is also a defender, especially on psychic planes.

Raphael, however, is the healer of psychic wounds, and of Air which represents the intellect, and he, therefore has a rightful place in this sphere.

The striving for knowledge can place us in danger, psychically, and it is good at these times to have mighty Michael on your side. Should these explorations result in psychic hurts, it is good to have Raphael. The archangel you invoke depends, again, on the work you are doing.

The Angels of Hod are the "Beni Elohim", literally "Sons of God/dess", but should be translated as "Children of God/dess". These are the forms for the energies represented by the Elohim, the Angels of Netzach.

These forms are not the transient, often illusory, thoughtforms of Yesod, but are "telesmic images", something very different. A telesmic image is a form that has been imbued by hundreds of years of use with special qualities and a kind of permanence. Every godform can be used as a telesmic image. You visualize the form strongly, establishing it firmly on the astral by concentration and giving of energy. When it is established and has become a worthy vessel for that Deity (or other figure) you wish to invoke, that particular energy will enter your image and it will become the God or Goddess.

Hod's Spiritual Experience is the "Vision of Splendor". Splendor in a great building, a pyramid, a vast desert, an affair of state, can bring awe, can be most impressive, even if it is not beautiful. It need not touch the heart. It does touch the mind. The Vision of Splendor reaches the mind in the same way that the Vision of Beauty Triumphant touches the heart.

The power of Shakespeare's plays, their words, their emotions, is beautiful; it touches the heart. The fact that they still do so after 400 years, the fact that a human, mortal mind was able to put words together in a way that they are still moving today, is splendid. Yet the experience is as important and moving as the Vision of Beauty Triumphant.

The Magical Image is the Hermaphrodite. At Hod and at Netzach, we have the pair of spheres closest to physical manifestation, and we have the bases of the Masculine and Feminine Pillars. We are as close to the division of the sexes as we can be without actually manifesting as such. The Hermaphrodite, being of both sexes, symbolizes that as well as symbolizing the sphere of male deities on the Feminine Pillar.

It is said that as man can fertilize woman on the physical plane, so does woman fertilize man on the spiritual plane. Therefore, the gods are not ill-placed on this sphere, for in contrast to Binah and Chokmah, with the energy of the "male" sphere fertilizing the female sphere, and the female sphere providing form, restriction, organization for the male energy, Hod is fertilized by Netzach, the female energizing the male, and the male "Mind" provides form for the female "Soul".

If the application of Mind as male and Soul as female offends you, why? Is one more important than the other? Does Soul advance and grow without the thoughts, ideas, the logic of Mind? Does the Mind grow and advance without the spark, the emotion, the wonder of Soul?

The "art therapy" I spoke of in the previous chapter, although in appearance dealing totally with Netzach, still contains a balance between Netzach and Hod. The creative energy is invoked and used to provide the impetus and inspiration for the artwork, but it is put into a form, a pattern, which is a function of Hod.

More than any other pair, Hod and Netzach are best understood by comparing them.

Occult books, grimoires, and studies, come under the jurisdiction of Hod. Netzach is natural magic, instinctive magic.

Hod is the text of a ritual, the form, while Netzach is the performance of the ritual and the energy given to it.

Hod is the drawn pentagram; Netzach, the flame when it is charged.

Netzach is sound. Hod is words, sound in pattern. (Mantras especially come under the jurisdiction of Hod.)

Netzach is concerned with Nature contact and elemental contacts; Hod with ritual magic and knowledge for the sake of knowledge.

Hod is the Lord of Books; Netzach the Lady of Nature. Hod is instinct; Netzach, emotion. Hod is Ceremonial Magic; Netzach, the traditional Craft.

Between Hod and Netzach is the Great Rite.

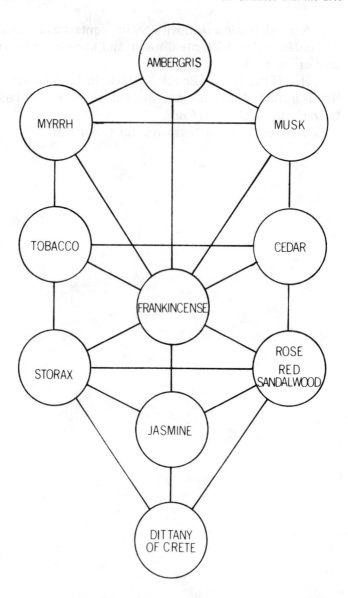

PERFUMES

CHAPTER 11

"AND THE WHITE MOON AMONG THE STARS"

We come to the sphere which just precedes physical being, Yesod, the "Foundation". Yesod is the sphere most easily reached from physical manifestation, just as its Planetary Attribution, the Moon, is the heavenly body most easily reached from Earth.

In a sense, we live in Yesod as constantly as we live in Malkuth, for Malkuth (the next sphere) is physical matter, but Yesod provides the life in that matter.

The attribution of the Moon to Yesod means that all Moon Deities belong in this sphere: Luna, Hecate, Diana, Hathor, Ganesha. The phases of the Moon reflect the faces of the Triple Goddess: Waxing, Full, Waning; Maiden, Mother, Crone. The Moon in waxing and waning phases does not truly grow or shrink. Moonrise after moonrise during the waxing moon, more of Her is revealed to us, parts of the Moon that were always there, but not illuminated. During the waning moon, more becomes hidden, moonrise after moonrise, until the Moon itself cannot be seen. Yet the physical Moon does not change during these phases. It presents to us, at all times, the same side, the same face. The phases are illusion, and Yesod is the Sphere of Illusion.

Yesod is the Akasha, the Astral, the Etheric Planes. It is in Yesod that we build our thoughtforms, or rather their images. We build these forms in Yesod and those images, if imbued with enough of our own energy, pull the energy into them from other spheres. Never forget, however, that the images in Yesod are just that—images. All our thought-forms are just images until energy enters them. The Mirror and the Moon are connected with Yesod for good reason; both reflect light and images. One of Yesod's titles is "The Treasurehouse of Images". These supposed forms can be very misleading, and the uninformed are often led astray by accepting them as the real thing.

For this among many reasons, the use of a symbolic system such as the Qabala is not only useful, but necessary. First, training the deeper levels for the mind to use the same symbols as the conscious can prevent a lot of misinterpretation. Secondly, the knowledge of the spheres beyond Yesod teaches us that the "images" we see are only symbols of that which is greater, that there is more to the "beyond" than the Astral Plane.

The Name of Power of Yesod is "Shaddai El Chai", usually translated "Almighty Living God". I prefer "Almighty Living One". It is an interesting name. "El" does mean "God" and "Chai" is "Life", but "Shaddai" means "breasts". I'm tempted to do a paragraph or two of pondering on this name, but I think I'll leave that to you. It would make a very good meditation.

Yesod is the sexual plane, and the fertility plane. It is in Yesod that the souls enter the body created for them. This falls under the jurisdiction of the angels of this sphere, the Aishim, "Souls of Fire".

Only one other author attributes these angels to Yesod; W. G. Gray. The rest attribute the Kerubim to this sphere, and the Aishim in the sphere to come. I have reasons for attributing the Kerubim to Malkuth, which I will explain in greater detail in the next chapter.

Just as different traditions of the Craft, and other similar beliefs, have their own attributions of the elements, their own view of the Lord and Lady, so do Qabalists often differ on these attributions to the sephiroth. All any of us can do is use the attributions which "feel" right to us. It well may be that when I've worked with Qabala another eight years, I'll make even more changes, or come to agree with those I differ with now. Any argument based on differences in attributions would be a waste of time. I tend to stick to the traditional attributions *unless* it feels wrong to me, or another seems more right.

The *right* attribution is one that seems instinctively so. For example, although every set of Tarot cards, and every book on ceremonial magic (except one) and many other witches contend that the weapon for Air is the Sword, and for Fire is the Wand. I, however, am an Air/Wand, Sword/Fire person and always have been. Fire *burns* a wand, and I can't feel that a weapon is appropriate if it can be destroyed by the element it is supposed to control.

That's just my opinion, however. Even some members of my coven are Air/Sword folks, and that is their privilege. These things are too personal for others to make a judgement on.

The Archangel of this sphere is Gabriel. You may be familiar with him as the Archangel of Water, but he is known also in the Christian mythos as the archangel who will blow the trumpet announcing Judgement Day. The Qabala may be the indirect source of this legend, just as it may be the source of the "old man on a throne" picture of God.

Yesod is not only the last step before physical manifestation, but the first step after the end of manifestation as well. The image of Gabriel standing over graves from which people are rising may be filtered down from the idea of the spirit leaving its now useless physical body.

Gabriel and his angels, the Aishim, guide spirits, or souls if you prefer, into their physical bodies before birth, and away from them after death. They are "in charge" of arranging or designing the forms which manifest in Malkuth, the physical plane. The matter itself is in Malkuth, but the forces which hold it together and give it life are Yesodic forces.

Many authorities place the Underworld and its Deities in Yesod, while I've placed them in Binah. Yesod, the first step after physical death, is where we would find ourselves after we leave our bodies behind. But this death of the body is only one ending when we cease to be incarnate. During our time between lives, we must suffer the death of the Personality, cease to be who we are in this life. I believe this would be a function of Binah.

Perhaps immediately after physical death we do find ourselves in a type of Underworld, one whose form is different for each of us: Heaven or Hell, the Summerland, the realm of Pluto. I would probably find myself trembling in the Hall of the Assessors, with Osiris and the Eater of Hearts waiting for me.

We would, immediately after death, be very much influenced by our present Personalities and their thoughts, so here we would remain, temporarily, until we are ready to continue.

The Vice of Yesod is Idleness. Teachers will recognize this. How often has a student who first worked very hard in his/her studies suddenly refused to put forth any further effort? This often passes, of course, and if it does not, the student does not advance . . . they remain in the Treasurehouse of Images, bemused by what they see, accepting it as truth. They are convinced they have found it all and do not need to travel further. It is to be hoped that the powers of Yesod continue to flow into them and bring forth the Virtue of Yesod, Independence.

One difference between Eastern and Western philosophies is the difference in the relationship between teacher and student. In an effort to escape from Self, an Eastern student is taught total blind obedience to the teacher. Within this philosophy is a valid teaching—you become one with all and begin by ceasing to think of the ego, the singular self.

In Western traditions, however, students are trained to learn within their own minds, to seek the Deity within, recognize it, grow toward it. Life is not avoided, it is sought out for the lessons it has to teach. One reaches for the Deity within. One conquers everyday life, instead of avoiding it. Independence, therefore, is a most desirable quality in a student. Questions, doubts, ideas and thoughts *should* flow into the mind of a student.

This time becomes a test for the teacher. In a sense, teachers are parents, and it is often difficult for a parent to allow the child to grow up. They feel a pang of loss when the children begin to think for themselves, develop minds of their own. The parent must let go, let the children make their own decisions and their own mistakes.

So often when a student and teacher first come together, the student hungers for knowledge, sits at the feet of the teacher, if only symbolically, and soaks in every word, every thought, every instruction. Teachers are human beings, and this is a wonderful feeling, this feeling of power. If we teachers have grown as *we* should have, we will allow them to grow, become adults in the Craft, give up the ego-boost of having them hang on our every word, depend on us for every spiritual thought.

We're human, we'll feel the pain of losing that, but

that can be replaced by a feeling of pride as our students move forward, upward, grow, perhaps even surpass us in knowledge.

It can be a joy, too, to observe the results of the Yesod Spiritual Experience, the "Vision of the Machinery of the Universe". I consider this one of the most strengthening, most comforting of all the experiences. This vision does not mean that the student will understand totally the Divine Plan, the Holy Workings of the Universe, but one who has had this experience knows that there is a plan, that the machinery exists. That cry of "Why?" into the darkness I spoke of in an earlier chapter is, in a sense, answered by this experience . . . not that you know why, but that you know there is a reason, you will know that of a certainty. You will know that things will be as they should, and that you will understand. You become aware that the Wheel of Life is *rolling*, not spinning. You will still experience the ups and downs of the Wheel, but you will know that every time you reach the bottom, you are further ahead than the last time; you are moving forward. Small trials become almost unimportant, large ones are analyzed for the lessons they contain.

Several characters in the novel, *Green Light*, by Lloyd C. Douglas have this experience. One of the characters says that he knows he is part of the Divine Plan, that delays are only red lights and that when it is time for him to move forward, he'll see the green light. The awareness that gives such comfort and, yes, even joy, to the people in this book can be none other than the Vision of the Machinery of the Universe.

How wonderful to know, in the depth of yourself, that we are all moving forward, together, as one. This is the greatest teaching of Yesod. Once *truly* felt, truly experienced, the Vice of Idleness must disappear, for you are carried forward by the wave of humanity struggling toward its source. Through the coming dark nights of the soul, that Vision can sustain you.

The Magical Image that will help you contact all that Yesod represents is a beautiful naked man, very strong. He represents the potential, the fertility of the sphere. A young fertile woman would not be inappropriate, but in the male figure, the potential for fertility is physically obvious. Use of the male figure also prevents any confusion with the Magical Image of the Netzach.

The potential expressed by this image becomes what we call reality in Malkuth.

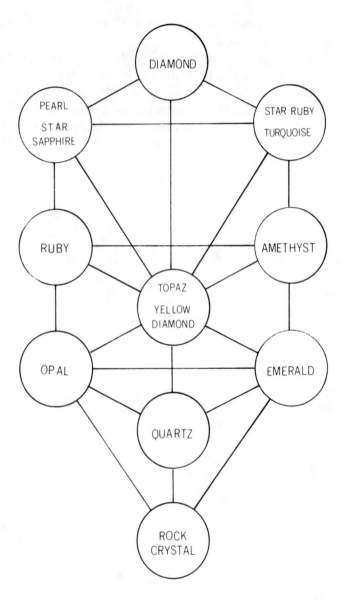

STONES

CHAPTER 12

"I AM THE BEAUTY
OF THE GREEN EARTH"

Before we discuss this sphere, I'd like to take a moment to discuss briefly the path between Yesod and Malkuth, the "32nd Path".

One of its symbols is Saturn, the Planetary Attribution of Binah, the idea of form. It is most appropriate to find a reflection of Binah on the path approaching physical manifestation, concrete form.

The color of this path is black. Many people who have "died" and been revived have reported the sensation of traveling through a dark tunnel. This fits perfectly with the symbology of traveling from the sphere of Malkuth, the physical world, to Yesod, by way of the 32nd Path.

We travel this path from Yesod to Malkuth, a world we have little difficulty understanding, the physical world, the world of manifestation. Malkuth means "The Kingdom". Its planet is, of course, the Earth, but Malkuth contains all that is physical and therefore, the solar systems, planets and galaxies.

Be careful to avoid any confusion of your "earths". There is the planet Earth, the element of Earth and the sphere of Malkuth, which includes both of the others.

The Deities of Malkuth are all Earth Deities, Corn or Grain Deities: Pan, Seb, Persephone, Ceres, etc.

Malkuth receives all the emanations of the other spheres, all the ideas, and potentials come together in "reality". For many, this is the only reality.

All spheres are equally holy, equally divine. We must not make the mistake of considering Malkuth a lesser sphere than the others. It is as vital a part of the Tree as Kether.

One analogy for the place of Malkuth on the Tree is to consider a light bulb. The electricity flows down one wire through the light bulb, producing light, then back through another wire to its source, just as the energy of Kether flows through the spheres to Malkuth, manifests and completes the circuit by returning to Kether.

It is said that the Tree is upside down, having its roots in Heaven. This means that Malkuth is the top of the Tree, not its bottom. The text from the *Sepher Yetzirah* reads: The Tenth Path is called the Resplendent Intelligence, because it is exalted above every head, and sits upon the Throne of Binah. This not only establishes Malkuth as the Top of the Tree, but expresses the presence of the Goddess in the physical world, and therefore its Divinity.

The refusal of many faiths to recognize the divinity in physical matter is the cause of most of the pathology, spiritual and physical, we encounter. "As above, so below." If Kether is holy, so then is Malkuth. If Malkuth is not holy, neither is Kether, and that is ridiculous. The physical world is not a corrupt creation, separate from its Maker who is now embarrassed by His/Her creation. We, and all around us, are an integral living part of our Lord and Lady; a vital part without which They would be incomplete.

Kether's Magical Image is a King. Malkuth's is "A

young queen, crowned and throned (or veiled, in some books). Crowned and throned . . . crowned and throned . . . the Crown of Kether and the Throne of Binah.

Kether is said to be entirely positive and Malkuth totally feminine, receptive to all other spheres. We come down the Tree from pre-being to physical being. Now, whether we are using this glyph or not, we are working back up the Tree to Kether, having learned and grown and become something more than we were through our experiences. We reach from this physical life to that which is our source. That reaching, that going forth is *positive*, so Malkuth is also masculine, or positive.

One of Malkuth's titles is the "Gate of Death", a little confusing because we enter Malkuth when we are *born*. However, we leave it when our body dies and we cease, temporarily, to have a physical existence. In that sense, it is the Gate of Death, but the term is also appropriate in another sense.

Before entrance into Malkuth, we are not incarnate, not bound by physical being. At birth as we know it, we leave behind all that we know, start again with minds bare of any knowledge. All we meet in Malkuth are strangers to us; we remember nothing of lives before or loved ones. Could not this be considered a form of death? Passing through this gate in either direction is both death and birth. At the death of the body, we rejoin our Greater Selves, recover our memories, our knowledge, rejoin those we have known and loved. Death becomes birth.

The Archangel of Malkuth is Sandolphon, the Approacher, and his angels are the Kerubim, the Strong.

In ceremonial magic, and in my Craft tradition, we deal with four other archangels in Malkuth, the Archangels of the Elements. They too have angels over which they rule, divisions of the Kerubim. The angels do not have names as such, but are signified by the symbols of the fixed

signs of the Zodiac. Raphael is the Archangel of Air, and
his angels are the ♒. Michael is the Archangel of Fire; his
angels, the ♌. Gabriel rules Water and the angels are signified by ♏. Over Earth is the Archangel Auriel, and his
angels, the ♉.

When these symbols are used to signify these angels,
they are called "kerubs". This is one of the reasons I place
the Kerubim in Malkuth rather than Yesod. The other is
taken from the Old Testament, which, although not the
sacred writings to me they are to the Christian Faith, are
still interesting from a Qabalistic point of view. The Old
Testament states that when Adam and Eve were driven
from Eden, a Kerub bearing a fiery sword was placed "at
the *Gate*" to prevent their return. Malkuth has no less than
three titles which refer to it as a Gate. The attribution of
the Kerubim therefore seems very fitting, very natural, and
very right to me.

The Name of Power of Malkuth is Adonai Ha Aretz,
"Lord of Earth". Again, the translation is masculine, and
inappropriate if Malkuth is entirely feminine. It will work
just as well with Adonath, Lady of Earth. If we are working
up the Tree, in meditation for example, Lord of Earth is
appropriate.

The Vice of Malkuth is "Inertia". . . an object at rest
tends to remain at rest. The Great Work, the way of life
which holds that we can shorten our time on the Wheel of
Life by deliberate growth, is a difficult one, and the first
step is the most difficult. Many are reluctant to take it. A
part of us, probably not a conscious part, knows the pain
and effort and frustration involved in the Work, and fights
against taking that first irretrievable step.

Once you have known the "Vision of the Holy Guardian Angel", you know that you must go forward through all
the dark nights ahead, and this Vision is the Spiritual Experience of Malkuth. This Holy Guardian Angel is your Inner

Self, your Greater Self, that of which you, in your present Personality, are a part. This is the "bright being" radiating love seen by so many who have been "dead" and returned to life.

This is the You that is aware of all your lives, all your pasts, your lessons, (learned and unlearned), your trials, your successes, your failures; your own Tree of Life of which you are a branch; the Real You, the Eternal You, the most holy, divine part of you. The Vision teaches that there is more than the Personality in which you are manifest. The simplest way to express this knowledge is a belief in reincarnation. *Now* is not all there is, not your only life. You have had, will have others. With this knowledge comes the understanding that there must be a reason for many lives, and eventually, the knowledge that this reason must be growth.

We know that growing up is difficult. "Growing pains" are very real. We can all look back in this life to the hurtful times, the despairing times, the agonizing times, and realize that we have become adults not only despite them, but because of them. Imagine how much greater is the pain involved in the greater growing of the spirit. All of us will grow, will return to our Source; it cannot be avoided. But some of us know that by deliberate work we can shorten this growing, and we chose the shorter and more arduous path. Once that decision is made and the first step taken, we cannot turn back, even if we try. It takes effort and determination to make that first step.

Once that step is taken, another problem arises. We are often confused by the many paths that lead forward, or seem to. When we search and choose the right one (and there is a different one for each), we've developed the Virtue of Malkuth, Discrimination.

In your list of correspondences, you'll find that the Perfume for Malkuth is Dittany of Crete. Dittany, when used as an incense, produces not only a distinctive odor, but also a tremendous amount of smoke. Again, on your list of correspondences, you'll see that the Magical Weapons of this sphere are the Magical Circle and the Triangle of Art. In ceremonial magic, the Magical Circle is a protective one and the Triangle of Art used to contain demons or whatever spirit one wished to conjure up. In order to maintain a physical manifestation, the entity must have some physical material from which to create a new form. The smoke of Dittany provides that.

I doubt you wish to conjure up any demons, but this bit of information can give you an inkling as to how certain attributions were made. Whatever the original reasons behind them, they have taken on greater power through constant use, and their meaning has grown.

"Playing" with the attributions of the Qabala is an excellent way to learn and absorb it. Search for Qabalistic symbolism around you. You might gain from playing a bit with the few Hebrew words you've learned so far. The comment on the "wheels" of Ezekiel is one example. Another is taking the sentence "Unless ye become as a little child, ye cannot enter the kingdom . . . " and substituting "Malkuth" for "kingdom". It means something entirely different that way, doesn't it?

We have reached the bottom (or top) of our Tree. The following chapters will provide further information on how to put it to use.

CHAPTER 13

THE FOUR WORLDS

Each sphere, and indeed the Tree itself, is divided into four levels, or worlds, symbolized by the Flashing Colors—one color, or combination of colors, for each world.

In Hebrew, these four worlds are:

Atziluth	—the Archetypal World
Briah	—the World of Creation (from the Hebrew for "giving shape")
Yetzirah	—the World of Formation (from the Hebrew for "forming")
Assiah	—the World of Manifestation (from the Hebrew for "completing")

These worlds each represent a level or type of energy as it manifests in the spheres. I prefer to use the following terms for these energies:

Atziluth	—Deity Force
Briah	—Archangel Force
Yetzirah	—Angelic Force
Assiah	—Planetary (or Elemental) Force

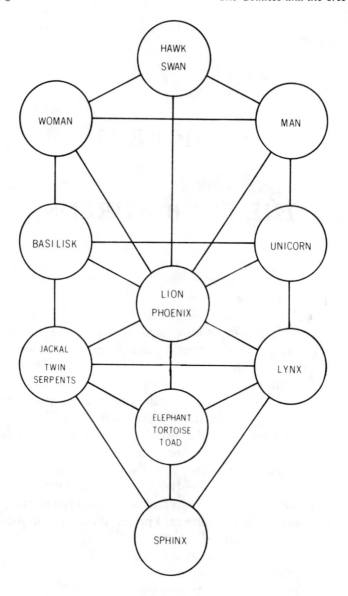

ANIMALS

The Deity Force represents the creative urge. The Archangel represents the creation of a concept. The Angel force produces the image, and the Planetary forces are the final manifestation.

The World of Assiah, often called the Mundane Chakras, include the powers symbolized by the planets and the circle of the Zodiac. The "Planetary" world in Malkuth is manifest in the four Mystic Elements.

These four worlds can be equated to the spiritual meanings of the quarterly sabbats.

Deity Force — Winter. It is at this season that the Sun is born. Although it is not obvious *on* the Solstice, the "direction" of the Sun has changed. To use the agricultural analogy, at this time of year, we consider and choose that which we wish to grow in the year to come. Key phrase: The seed is chosen.

Archangel Force — Spring. At this season, when the Earth bursts into life, we plant that which we wish to grow. Key phrase: The seed is planted.

Angelic Force — Summer. In the Summer, that which we have planted has (we hope) sprouted and grown, and, although its growth is not yet complete, we can see the form it will take. Key phrase: That which was planted takes form.

Planetary Force — Autumn. It is at this season that the growth is completed, and we harvest that which we have planted and grown, that which we have earned. What was begun in Winter is manifest in Autumn. Key Phrase: The seed is gathered.

Yet another way to view the flow of energy from one world to another, from creative urge to manifestation, can be that of a journey:

Deity Force: The direction is chosen.

Archangel: The first step is taken, the journey has begun.

Angelic: The journey continues.

Planetary: The destination is reached.

The Deity Force says: "There should be a way to clean up that dirt". The Archangel says: "The best way would be to have something suck it up. The Angels produce the design. The Planetary Powers produce a vacuum cleaner.

The Deity Force says: "Millions of televisions and with only one use. That's such a waste of knowledge and technology".

The Archangel Force says: "Well, we'll have to figure out another way to use them. The Angels go to work on it, and the Planetary Powers produce Pac-Man!"

I thought: "Too bad so many pagans don't know how wonderful Qabala is". Then, I thought, "I should tell them". My next thought was "I could write a book".

VOILA!

CHAPTER 14

CREATING YOUR OWN TREE

Before you do any real work with the Tree of Life, I would suggest you create your own personal Tree. Having it in easy sight as you study and/or meditate will facilitate your learning and absorption of the Qabala. The Tree itself makes an excellent focus for meditation. My own Tree is before me now, as it has been always when I was writing.

I encourage you to make a big production out of the creation of your Tree. Make the drawing and coloring a ritual. If this Tree is to be used by a group, the group should participate; each adding color to each sphere, discussing the meaning of the sphere, vibrating the Name of Power, and whatever else will make the ritual meaningful.

If the sphere is for personal use, make it a private ritual, pondering the spheres as you apply the color, vibrating the Deity name, etc.

The effects of this ritual will be enhanced if you will use a medium in which colors can be mixed rather than crayon or felt tip pens. Use the clearest, cleanest, brightest

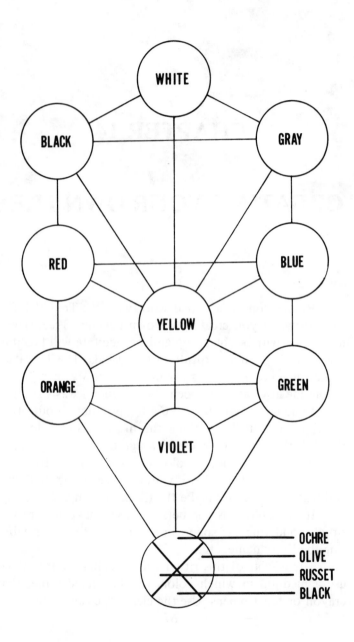

colors you can obtain. As we discussed in the section on the Four Worlds, we use the Archangel scale of colors.

Kether's Archangel color is "Pure white brilliance". Granted, it is difficult to find a paint to express "brilliance", so use the whitest white available, perhaps Zinc White. This will serve even better if the paper you are using is not quite white . . . a cream or off-white will make the Zinc White stand out even more.

All colors are included in white light. All that is to come, that is to be, all the significance of the other colors are within white. How much greater then is held within "pure white brilliance". Whatever paint you use, it will only be a poor approximation of Kether's true meaning, but your very consideration of this as you color the sphere of Kether will be important.

Chokmah is a clean, cloud-like gray . . . clouds forming out of the invisible water vapor in the sky, becoming visible.

Binah is black, preferably a flat or matte black. Black is the absence of all color. No rays are returned, nothing is bounced back. Black receives all as Binah is the epitome of receptivity.

Use a pure blue for Chesed, an equally clear red for Geburah, and a golden, gleaming sun-yellow for Tiphareth.

We move now from the primary colors to those which must be mixed. Emerald green is the proper color for Netzach, pure blue and pure yellow. As you mix, striving for the exact color you desire, consider the significance of the two colors and the meaning of the mixture.

Hod is orange, a mixture of red and yellow.

Yesod is Violet, the blending of pure red and pure blue.

Now to Malkuth which has four colors, usually given as citrine, russet, olive and black.

I had some difficulty understanding these colors until I talked to an artist whose knowledge of mixing colors clarified it for me.

Olive is created by mixing red and green; russet by mixing orange and blue. AHA!

Then comes black, the same color as Binah. We are reminded that Malkuth sits on the throne of Binah, and the color at the base of Malkuth is black. There is a difference, however. In Binah you are dealing with light, and there black absorbs all light rays. In Malkuth, we are dealing with the physical world, with paint, and therefore with the presence of all colors. If you use a glossy paint, you will differentiate easily between the two aspects of black.

"Citrine" is not so easily dealt with, and it is with the deepest respect and apologies to Dr. Regardie, Dion Fortune, Mr. Gray, Mr. Butler, Mr. Knight, and Mr. Crowley that I submit the following: Citrine doesn't work.

Olive is a mixture of the three primary colors with blue predominating; russet a mixture of the three with red predominating. It follows that the quarter expressed as "citrine" should be a mixture of the three with yellow predominating.

"Citrine" is "lemon-yellow" achieved by adding a touch of blue to yellow—there is no red. The color for this quarter, the results I get when I actually *mix* the colors in this proportion is "ochre", a mixture of purple and yellow.

I can think of three possible explanations for the attribution of citrine:

1. A mistranslation somewhere along the line. A scholar of the Hebrew language might know of a word for "lemon yellow" and a word for a shade of "yellow brown" that are similar.

2. Lemons were, once upon a time, a very different color.

3. It's one of those cute little curves the writers of old used to confuse the uninitiate.

In every other correspondence, I agree with at least one of the experts, but in this one I must differ. The choice is yours, as always.

The paths have their own colors, and the scales for these can be found in many a good Qabala text. You may add these at a later time, but for now, let it be. Spend some time with your Tree, meditate on its total significance.

Having this Tree before you whenever you are working with Qabala or studying it will be of immeasurable help to you in experiencing and understanding it. After all, the original Qabalists had only this to work from, and look at what they accomplished!

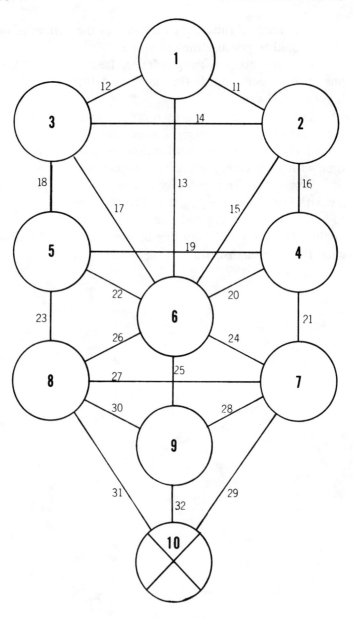

THE PATHS

CHAPTER 15

"THOU WHO THINKEST TO SEEK ME"

You have your own Tree of Life before you and are ready to do some work with this wonderful tool. How do you use it? In a hundred, a thousand ways, my friend, but I can share only a few.

The Qabalistic Cross
This simple exercise should be the first thing you memorize. It is a good way to prepare for ritual, meditation, or simply to clear away negativity. I've used it as a minor protective rite to keep away negativity being sent by others.

Stand quietly a moment, breathing deeply and rhythmically, and still your thoughts.

Now, imagine you are growing larger and larger with each breath. Your head touches the ceiling, passes through it. You are now looking at the roof, at all the roofs in your neighborhood.

Now the city is stretched out before you, the state, the continent.

The spinning earth is below you, tiny and growing tinier.

You are larger than the solar system, the galaxy, all of creation.

Imagine now that just above the crown of your head is a brilliant, swirling sphere of light. Don't force it. Let it be there.

Vibrate the word "Atoh" (Thou art), as you touch your forehead.

Picture a beam of light flowing from the sphere down to your feet as you point to them and vibrate "Malkuth". The light forms another sphere, half above and half below the ground.

Touch your right shoulder and visualize another sphere forming there as you vibrate "Ve Geburah".

Draw your hand across your chest, picturing a beam of light following your hand and touch your left shoulder, vibrating "Ve Gedulah" as a fourth sphere of light forms at your shoulder.

You now have a cross of light extending from your head to your feet and from your right shoulder to your left.

Clasp your hands at the intersection of the cross. Vibrate "Le Olahm" as a fifth sphere of light forms around your hands. This sphere continues to expand until it fills your entire aura.

Stand a moment in this light and vibrate "Amen".

A version that is a bit more pagan is the following. It has not as yet been used enough to build up the power the original has, but it has a nice effect.

Directing your words to the Lord and Lady, visualize the sphere above your head, touch your forehead and say:

"Thou art"

The Kingdom (point to feet)

The Strength (touch right shoulder)

The Mercy (touch left shoulder)

And the Love (clasp hands)
Forever (sphere of light expands)
So mote it be.

Meditation

Before discussing the various Qabalistic meditations, it might be worthwhile to discuss briefly the two types of meditation. It has been my experience that students are aware of only one type, Passive Meditation.

This is the most common type of meditation and benefits both spirit and body. Concentration on a focal point, a candle, a mantra or a mandala to the extent that all else is "blanked out" brings rest to the body and mind, and opens the spirit to the inflow of spiritual energies.

Active meditation is quite different. It might be called "concentrated contemplation".

You should begin your meditation with the passive type to still the mind and narrow your concentration. Then you move on to your active phase.

If you are using a magical image, perhaps a "young queen, crowned and throned", begin by visualizing this as completely and with as much detail as possible. When the visualization is as complete as you can make it, see what thoughts, what questions come to you.

"Walk" around the image, look at it from all angles. What do you feel when you look at it? Follow each train of thought to see where it leads you. If your mind wanders too far afield, lead it gently back by vibrating the Name of Power of the sphere and/or going carefully over the image detail by detail.

If the image should begin to change, watch. After a bit, if this seems to be a matter of lessened concentration rather than developing ideas, re-firm your mental image.

If you can, it is effective to *become* the image, see through the eyes of the young queen. Think her thoughts.

Active meditation is not only a learning process, but an invocation of the energies represented by the subject of the meditation, and its effects can be far-reaching.

The Tree has many other subjects for meditations: the symbols of the spheres, the Deities attributed to each, as well as the planets. You can contact the archangels by imagining yourself surrounded by their colors, or, as Gareth Knight suggests, picturing a pillar of energy, with the color swirling in it.

Rising On The Planes

One method of experiencing the Tree is known as "Rising on the Planes". There are several methods for doing this. Mine is as follows:

Imagine yourself surrounded by the planetary colors of Malkuth (black, rayed with yellow). The swirling colors change gradually to the Angelic colors (ochre, russet, olive and black, flecked with gold). The gold flecks disappear, leaving the Archangel colors. After awhile, your aura becomes pure yellow. Don't remain in this color too long— let the color change to citrine flecked with azure, the planetary colors of Yesod. These colors change gradually to purple, then violet, then indigo.

What you have done here with the use of color is to move from the Assiatic world of Malkuth to the Atziluth of Yesod. If you wish to continue to another sphere, choose the sphere, surround yourself with its planetary color and continue. When you have gone as high as you wish, drop back to the Archangel color and remain there as long as you like. When you have completed your meditation, return by reversing your visualization.

Astral Temples

Another method for concentrating on a sphere is to build an "astral temple" for the proper sphere and do your meditation "there". Look at the list of correspondences in Appendix I and use those symbols to design your temple. Build it by imagining your temple, building it in your mind. You can even "construct" it piece by piece. It will become a very real place when you've worked on it and in it long enough. You can combine this meditation with others, perform the other methods in your astral temple.

Suggested descriptions of the temples of Malkuth, Yesod, Hod and Netzach will be found in Appendix II. These are the descriptions I use; you may add to or change them if it suits you, as long as you keep the symbolism within the proper correspondence for the spheres.

Mantras

Mantras are somewhere between active and passive meditation, although a bit closer to passive. You combine rhythmic breathing with a phrase mentally repeated.

For example, let us say you wish to work with Yesod, to learn more about the sphere, or develop your divination skills.

Choose an eight-syllable phrase; in this case, we'll use "O Silver Moon, help me to see".

Begin by getting comfortable and relaxing. Start breathing in a gentle, four-beat rhythm. In - 2 - 3 - 4, Out - 2 - 3 - 4, In - 2 - 3 - 4, Out - 2 - 3 - 4.

It won't take long for your body to take up the rhythm. (This rhythmic breathing is very good for you and can be done almost any time, anywhere).

When this rhythm becomes natural, mentally accompany the breathing with the mantra:

In 2   3   4   Out 2 3 4
O sil - ver moon,   Help me to see.

When this becomes easy for you to do without much concentration, you add the visualization of inhaling the Yesod Archangel color. With each inhalation you draw in whirling, swirling violet light. It enters your lungs, and you can feel the energy of that light being absorbed. As you continue to breathe, mentally chant and inhale the energy-filled light, you will feel the energy enter your bloodstream, and begin to circulate through your body with the energy of Yesod. Eventually your physical body and your aura will be full of this whirling, swirling violet light.

When you are ready to end the meditation, continue the breathing; picture the violet light in your aura becoming absorbed into your physical body. Let the violet color fade, although the energy remains.

After a moment or two, cease your chant.

Sit quietly, still breathing rhythmically. If thoughts come to you, make notes on them.

The breathing and mental chanting can be done almost any time. I use a chant when I'm walking or gardening.

Magical Work

The meditation methods detailed above can be incorporated into specific magical work. You may add your own circle casting and closing, invocations and prayers, etc.

If your work pertains to a specific sphere, gather what you can of the proper correspondences. For example, if you wish to do an invocation of Thoth, the great teacher, you could cover your altar with an orange cloth, use orange candles, burn storax, use an opal in the rite, have a statue or picture of the god you wish to contact. Since the god in this case is Thoth, a statue or picture of an ibis will do as well.

Hod's number is eight. You can incorporate this into the ritual in the form of knocks, a number of candles, an invocation repeated eight times. Use your imagination to make the ritual truly yours. Use one of the meditation methods to contact the powers represented by Hod and proceed with your work.

Spell Casting

The following is a method of spell-casting developed by the coven where I received my training. It can be used for any kind of a spell.

First, decide which sphere is the appropriate one for your work. Choose a candle in the Archangel color of that sphere.

Sit or stand, holding your candle, and fill your aura with the brilliant Deity light of Kether. Quickly change it to the Archangel color and dwell on that for a moment. Proceed to the Angel color, then the planetary color. (This is the reverse of the Rising on the Planes.)

If the sphere in which your work is centered is above Tifareth, continue through the spheres in order. If it is below Tifareth, it is best to go through Tifareth instead of taking a short cut. This will insure that you remain balanced. When you reach the sphere you wish to use, pause briefly at the Deity color and vibrate the Name of Power a few times. Try to emanate the adoration and love you feel for Deity in all forms.

Change to the Archangel color, greet the Archangel and ask his help. Speak of or concentrate on the goal of your spell. Continue down the tree by the use of the colors.

When you reach the Archangel color of Yesod, (Yes, *do* go through Yesod) pause and form a picture of your goal, your desire, as clearly and as strongly and with as much detail as you can.

Continue down through Malkuth and light your candle to signify the transference of your thought form to physical reality.

Repeat each day as necessary, using the same candle. Let it burn a certain amount each day, and extinguish it with the thought that it continues to burn on other planes. As often as you can during the day, add energy to your thought form by picturing it again.

A special note: Hod is always reached through Chesed and vice versa (Hod . . . "has no root . . . save in the hidden places of Gedulah"). Therefore, it is correct to go from Chesed through Tifareth to Hod instead of taking the long way around.

For healing, it is permissible to go straight down the Middle Pillar, from Kether to Tifareth to Yesod to Malkuth.

The Tarot

Although the Tarot was not applied to the Tree until comparatively recently, (the last few centuries) the two do fit together rather nicely.

The Major Arcana of the Tarot has 22 cards, one for each path on the Tree. The Minor Arcana has four suits of 13 cards each, Ace through ten, and four court cards.

One card of the Major Arcana is, of course, applied to each of the 22 paths. The Aces are in Kether, the two's in Chokmah, the three's in Binah and so forth.

The court cards are related to the four letters of the holy name, JHVH.

Other than divination, the Major Arcana cards have at least two uses in working the Qabala. They are excellent subjects for meditation in themselves, and they can be used as doors to the paths between the spheres. In Appendix II, you will see the doors in the temples marked with the name of a Tarot Trump. (NOTE: Most authorities seem to agree with Crowley who, in a meditation, was told that "Tzaddi is not the Star". Tzaddi is the Hebrew letter given to the path between Yesod and Netzach. Crowley decided to place the Emperor there and move the Star to the Emperor's place. I have not as yet come to agree with Crowley, and so have retained the traditional attribution of "The Star" on Tzaddi. It has always worked for me. If you should feel more comfortable with Crowley's attribution, by all means use it.

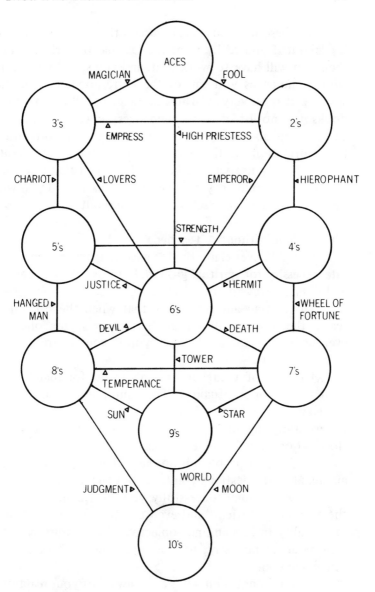

TAROT

All these methods can be used effectively on surface levels, but if you really want the Qabala to work for you, then you will have to work at it, and you start by *memorizing* as much as you can of the correspondences of the spheres. It is all very well to have a shelf full of reference books, but no list of correspondences, however complete, can accomplish what your own mind can do in correlating the information on different levels in different ways. Your mind can only use what it has retained. Get that information into your memory on a permanent basis, and you will be surprised, nay, *amazed* at what comes out.

The Student Without A Teacher

I would never claim that an earthly teacher is an absolute necessity for spiritual growth, but it is certainly easier, and in many ways more effective.

There is an ancient saying that when the student is ready, the teacher will appear. It is a true saying; one will eventually be made available to you if you are truly open to being taught.

The lack of a teacher is not an excuse for abandoning your search for spirituality. (The temptation to do so may be a symptom of the Vice of Malkuth, Inertia). By all means study, meditate, work, but be open to a teacher if the right one should come to you.

The biggest problem is not lack of guidance or lack of answers to the questions you have, but lack of objectivity.

To work alone successfully you must concentrate on the extremely difficult and even painful development of a rare quality in humankind—objectivity. You must learn to view yourself honestly, to step aside and see yourself as others see you.

If you do not, you will not be aware of your reactions to the influx of energies of the various spheres as they occur. I've mentioned one such reaction above, the Inertia of Malkuth. If you do not recognize it, you will not be able to push yourself out of it.

One technique which might help you develop that objectivity is to work on the development of your magical personality.

The first step in doing so is to choose a new name, a traditional step in many pagan traditions. Your new name represents the "perfected" you—the person you are striving to be, the best part of your present Self.

Many people choose the name of a god or goddess, one which symbolized the qualities they are reaching for. Some choose names of mythological figures they admire, or fictional characters. (Two members of my group have names from Tolkien.) Others make up a name that sounds good to them, that *feels* like them, or they choose a name they've always liked.

Take your time in making this choice. If you decide to change it later, you may, (we all change as we grow and our names can reflect this) but the better suited your name is to you now, the more effective will be its use.

Once you've chosen a name (let's say it is George), start thinking of George as the mature you, and your everyday name as the younger part.

I am not advocating that you develop a split personality. Both names are *you*, but different views, different aspects of yourself. You can be "Mommy" or "Daddy" to your children, "Son" or "Daughter" to your parents, Harry or Harriet to your friends, without being three different people. You can be George *and* Harry without being schizoid.

When you are meditating, spell-casting, or performing a ritual, think of yourself as George. Leave behind jealousy, anger, and all other types of negativity, bringing only the best of yourself into your circle. That's the first step.

The second is to practice seeing things from different

points of view. Many of us do this often if we have developed any understanding of others at all. We see things from another's point of view, realize why they followed a certain course of action, understand and forgive. Some can even see, understand and forgive when they themselves have suffered from the other person's actions.

Spend some time *trying* to see things as others see them. If a co-worker snapped at you without apparent reason, try to understand why. Was she tired? Was she ill? Did someone else snap at her? Did *you* snap at her first? Were you being irritating? Was she worried? Use your imagination and your intelligence.

Then apply that to yourself, being as objective as you can by having George try to understand Harry. "Harry, why did you yell at so-and-so today?" If Harry's only reason was that he felt like it, that's a lousy reason and he needs a serious talking to.

If Harry answers, "Because so-and-so was right, and I didn't want to admit it, so I yelled", that's still a lousy reason, but an understandable one, a human one. So is "What he said hurt, and I didn't want him to know it".

George should congratulate Harry on his honest answer, and Harry should promise to do better. If Harry insists that his reasons were valid and he fully intends to do what he wants to, he hasn't learned a thing. However, if this were truly the case, Harry wouldn't be the kind of person who is trying to grow. Harry is still covering up the fact that he's wrong (or hurt). Why on Earth, (or any other plane) should Harry try to hide from himself? Because he's human, and if he admits he wasn't justified in his anger, his own opinion of himself will suffer.

Give yourself the same love, understanding and forgiveness you would give anyone else, but don't let yourself get away with it. If you never reveal your true, imperfect self to anyone else in the world, you must not hide from you! In spiritual growth it is imperative that you learn to be honest with yourself. If you do not admit faults, you will never work to change and you will *not* grow, except in your ability to lie to yourself.

I've placed such an emphasis on this because if you do not have a teacher to observe you, you will not be aware of your changes unless you have learned to observe and be truthful with yourself.

If you manage to break the Inertia of Malkuth, all well and good. After Malkuth comes Yesod, the Sphere of Illusion. Suddenly, it is all so clear! You can see beyond the horizon, know the future, solve everybody's problems. *You* don't have any problems. You are all-seeing, all-knowing, all-powerful. WOW! You can see everybody's faults (you don't have any of those either, having by some cosmic means attained instant perfection). Teacher? Who needs a teacher? You've got it all right at your fingertips.

In other words, you are the magical equivalent of a first-year psychology student who, having learned the terms and symptoms for psychological malfunctions, believes himself immune to them.

When you reach this exalted state, become a semi-to-moderately instant adept, do me a small favor. Spend a few moments meditating on Joan Grant's interpretation of one of the questions asked by the 42 Assessors of Egyptian mythology:

HAST THOU SEEN THY GIANT SHADOW ON THE
WALL AND THOUGHT THYSELF MIGHTY?

You can see the problems of studying without a teacher. They are not insurmountable, but your path can be very difficult, painful and disheartening without a teacher. Working *with* a teacher can be difficult, painful and disheartening too, but it is easier to bear with the support and understanding of an experienced teacher.

Do what you can on your own, but be open to your

teacher when he/she comes. Work magically for that arrival.

If you decide to do a spell for a teacher, using the form of spell-casting contained in this chapter, the sequence is: Kether to Chokmah to Binah to Chesed to Tifareth to Hod. Use an orange candle, pause at Hod and vibrate the Deity name, and greet the archangel, etc. At Yesod, you visualize yourself being taught, continue to Malkuth and light your candle.

I urge you to make this attempt. And when you do find that you've been led to a teacher, use the Qabala to decide whether this is your teacher or not.

In my opinion, a teacher should have had at the very least the Vision of the Machinery of the Universe and preferably the Vision of the Beauty Triumphant. Ideally, a teacher should have had both Tifareth experiences, but these are not always attained.

Having experienced these visions, a good teacher should have a basic optimism about life, a belief that there is a direction, a purpose. None of us are optimistic 100% of the time, but this basic security in the workings of the Universe should be a pre-requisite.

Take your time, as I'm sure the teacher will take his/hers. If you are not comfortable with the teacher or the group, and it seems a serious discontent, look further. The first teacher is not always the one for you.

Until you find *your* teacher, work alone and carefully. May the Goddess guide and bless you.

CHAPTER 16

QABALA FOR TEACHERS AND GROUPS

As a teacher, you have to be a scholar, psychologist and spiritual advisor. You are expected to know all the answers, handle every problem, provide comfort and consolation. In addition to that, you must prepare classes, direct rituals and keep the group working together peacefully.

Qabala cannot solve all your problems, but it can make you a better teacher by helping you to recognize, and even predict the phases your students go through by giving you the proper techniques to guide your people through these phases.

The use of the Tree within my own tradition might suggest to you ways in which you can use it with your own students.

We have five "grades" which precede the First Degree. With the exception of the first grade, Neophyte, each of these is related to a specific sphere on the Tree, and to a specific element.

During Neophyte, a student is taught the basics of

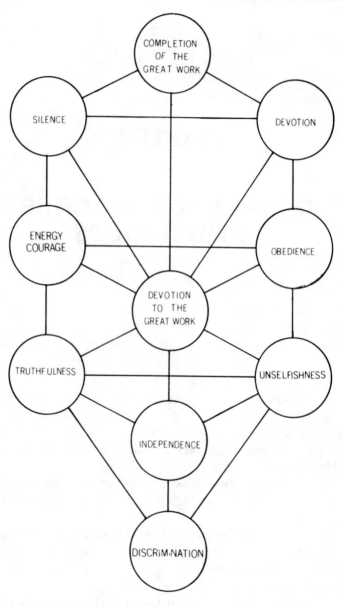

VIRTUES

ritual, the techniques and meditations we use, so that they may attune themselves to the energies of the group. Here we also teach the most basic things about the elements, the building of a magic circle, etc. Once these have been learned, we begin the true trek up the Tree.

Our elemental initiations begin with the Earth Grade, the Sphere Malkuth. In our Earth initiation, we invoke the element of Earth, so that during a student's time in this grade, the forces invoked bring forth problems which require work. In Earth grade, these are usually problems dealing with the physical plane: health, money, certain relationships, etc.

During the entire training program and beyond, the teachers in our tradition observe the students, pay attention to their growth, their advancement (or lack of it) and make a special effort to be aware of the student's reactions to the various forces brought into play.

For example, no matter how anxious to learn, how sincere a student is, there comes a time in Earth grade when they cannot get going. It's difficult for them to concentrate on their studies, so many things are allowed to interfere. Inertia, the vice of Malkuth has set in. We have learned to be patient, keep encouraging them, and if necessary, administer a little kick to the other side of their laps, (psychically speaking, of course) to get them moving again. The second law of inertia is that an object in motion tends to stay in motion. Once they get started, they'll be fine.

The second step is Air Grade, Yesod. (The Middle Pillar is the Air Pillar). Again, the element invoked insures that the student will work on problems appropriate to the force of Air, and the sphere.

When a student begins to work in Air, the Vice of Idleness sets in. It is at this point that many students fade away from the group, and often the Craft, altogether. They often decide they've learned it all, you have nothing to teach them, they have no further need of instruction for you. (See the discussion on Yesod's vice.) This may seem a strange way for Idleness to manifest, but if they are instant adepts, have achieved instantaneous cosmic consciousness, they won't have to do all that horrible studying and hard work, will they? The Sphere of Illusion makes it easy for them to convince themselves.

Some of them will make it through this stage and continue up the Tree. Many won't. Let them go. They may return at a later time, embarrassed and repentent. Welcome them home, and move forward. If not, your path was not theirs and your group is better off without them.

There is a type of student who never makes it past Yesod. They go from group to group, giving the impression of a sincere desire to learn. What they really want is recognition of their incredible spiritual prowess, in the form of rapid advancement upward within the group. When that is not forthcoming, they leave, fuming that they've been "at this for ten years and know more than the damned teacher!"

Perhaps some day, they'll realize that years mean nothing if they are spent bouncing up and down the 32nd path. You can spend ten years as a freshman in college— that does not earn a degree.

The Qabala is not studied until Air in our tradition, although many Qabalistic techniques are used before then. You should see the "Aha!" expressions as they recognize the significance of a meditation or chant they've been using.

Water Grade is Hod, and a student's work here is accompanied first by the Vice—Dishonesty—and finally the Virtue, Truthfulness.

You won't have any trouble getting them to study— the problem will be to get them to do anything else! They'll be very concerned with "book knowledge" at this point, and with "form".

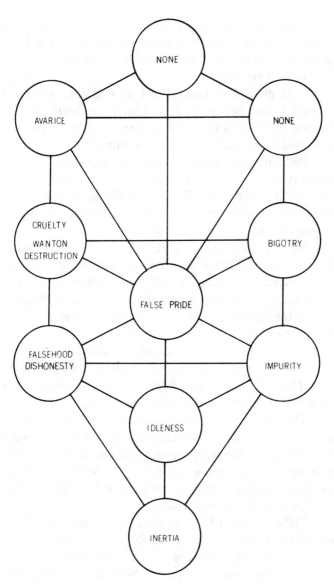

VICES

They may write very detailed, very precise, wonderful rituals, with no concern whatsoever for the "spark" and energy needed to make a ritual an effective one.

They'll get over it.

Netzach is Fire Grade, and all hell breaks loose, for Netzach is the Sphere of Emotion. Talk about "letting it all hang out!" This is a time to keep a tight rein on a student, placing special emphasis on ethics, etc.

Suddenly, the spark that was missing in their spells and rituals is there. Everything begins to work better. Remember that Netzach is a reflection of Geburah, and students get a mini-Vision of Power here, without having gone through the balancing of Tifareth.

One of the studies in Fire Grade is the writing of rituals. This concentration on Form, a Hodic quality, will help them regain a balance. You'll know things have calmed down when the Virtue of Unselfishness comes through.

After Fire Grade, we give the First Degree.

The experienced teachers among you will have realized at this point that these various phases sound familiar. Their students have gone through these stages in their growth, as indeed have the teachers, *whether or not you have ever seen the glyph of the Tree of Life or read a book on Qabala!*

These phases can be seen in other aspects of life, not just in the spiritual. A young High Priest I know was bemoaning the actions of some members of his group who have apparently been amused by the Sphere of Illusion. We discussed these theories and the light bulb coming on over his head was almost visible!

"When I was 17" he said, "I hit the sphere of Illusion and thought I knew everything. Boy, was I wrong!"

Mark Twain expressed it best when he remarked that he'd been disgusted, at 17, with the ignorance of his father, and four years later was amazed at the amount the old man had learned in such a short time.

At this point, the students have made a strong effort to work on all planes which deal with the Personality, on all four Elements within. This is not to say they will never need to tread these paths again. We all travel them many times, but a student who has reached First Degree has made a tremendous effort toward growth and balance.

When and if a student approaches Second Degree—Tifareth—the Vice of False Pride presents itself. The student is changing into a teacher and can be disgustingly aware of how much he or she has learned and grown. They are equally unaware of how much learning and growing remains. This is known as the "Pompous Ass Stage". A student at this level behaves in a very superior manner toward less advanced students (and even to the teacher) and is given to such patronizing statements as "I won't even try to explain it to you because you are not capable of understanding". This is obviously not the proper attitude for a teacher. When they have calmed down a bit and developed the attitude of sharing, of helping, they are ready to become teachers.

Between first and second degree is one of the many "dark nights of the soul" we encounter in spiritual work. Your guidance, comfort and help are greatly needed here.

During all these growing phases, the Qabala can be used to guide a student. You cannot teach them the Mysteries, but you can lead them to their own awarenesses, through the use of Magical Images, symbols, etc., inherent in the Qabala. Even if you use only the Magical Images, you'll make great strides, and so will they.

A special hint, if you do use the Tree as a guide. Just as you cannot leave a room completely without entering another, so a student often cannot complete the work in one sphere unless he moves to the next. If a student seems stuck in a sphere, move him/her forward by suggesting meditations on the sphere to come.

Specific problems which occur at any stage outside the normal difficulties that come with the energies invoked can be helped with the use of the Tree. When a problem becomes apparent, you can suggest work on the sphere which will counteract the difficulty. If a student is too dry, too logical (if that's possible—Mr. Spock wouldn't think so), too wrapped up in book knowledge, work on Netzach would be helpful. One ruled by emotions could use work on Hod. Work with Yesod will help the intuition and memory. Memory can also be helped by work on the 32nd path.

The information in Appendix III shows the spheres that will help with other problems.

Group Meditations

While personal meditations are not only encouraged but insisted upon in our tradition, group meditations are an important part of our training program.

The "Mantra" meditation is an effective group exercise as well as a solitary one, and fits easily into a ritual. If you have a small group, you can prepare a tape with the mantra repeated rhythmically for about ten minutes. Played as a background, it will help the students keep the chant and rhythm going as you instruct them on the visualization.

If you have a large group, two volunteers can chant the mantra quietly. With two, the chant remains constant because the chanter has to breathe.

One way to expose your students to the energies of the spheres is to conduct your classes in the astral temple of that sphere. Four such temples are described in Appendix II.

Describe the temple slowly to the class, letting them share in the visualization.

Conduct your class as usual, pausing once or twice to go over the visualization again. As your student's skills in visualization develop, there will be no need to repeat the description.

When the class is over, all of you should see the temple fading away to be replaced by the "real" location.

Rituals

As we are all aware, different rituals have different meanings and therefore use different forms of energy. A High Priestess or High Priest directs and controls the energies brought into the rite. The Qabala provides a very simple way of bringing into the circle the precise energy of the exact aspect of the Lord and/or Lady you wish to use.

Let us suppose you are performing a Moon Rite, New or Full. You have a group that is not too advanced, and you do not wish to draw the full force of the Goddess at her most impersonal, unknowable aspect. You want the gentle, loving power of the Moon.

After you've created your circle, picture the Tree before you (you can use a picture if you like) and imagine an influx of power from the Ain Soph to Kether. The energy flows down the Tree, sphere by sphere, until it reaches Yesod. At this point, see the violet colored energy filling your circle with Moon power. You are now ready to continue your rite, in a circle filled with the energy of the Sphere of the Moon.

A more advanced group whose visualization skills have developed can handle a slightly different method. Let them share the visualization with you, but this time fill the circles with the colors of Malkuth, starting with the planetary colors and working up through the Four Worlds. When you reach the Deity color, let the whole group see the Circle moving toward Yesod, entering it, and conduct the remainder of your circle in the Sphere of the Moon.

You'll feel a difference in the two rituals.

If you have a specific purpose other than worship,

one which requires other than Moon energy, start as I have
described, but fill the circle with the color of the proper
sphere in the first method, or move your circle to the
sphere as in the second. A healing rite would use energy
drawn from Tifareth, for example. The circle would be
filled with a sun-yellow light.

In Appendix VI, you'll find a rite using both Qabalistic
and Craft symbolism. The energies of four spheres and the
energies of all the elements are invoked, in order to cure
dissension between two members of a circle. A study of
this rite shows how easily the two can be intertwined.

The more you study and use the Qabala, the more
ideas you will find. As you grow, the Tree grows. There is
an unending source of knowledge, guidance, strength and
joy in the Tree of Life, and it is available to you, if only
you wish to have it.

CHAPTER 17

CONCLUSION

The symbolism of the Qabala is all around us, if we will look and see. Unintentionally, the world arranges itself qabalistically.

A traffic light goes from green (Netzach, Pillar of Force) to yellow (Tifareth, the Mediator, on the Middle Pillar) to red (Geburah, Pillar of Restriction).

Trees are green in their expansive cycle, and change to reds and oranges in their Geburah cycles.

I have friends of another tradition who feel that the most common arrangement of the elements in a circle (Fig. 1) are "ceremonial magic" attributions, and prefer the order in Figure 2. I do, of course, respect their beliefs and differences, but I must give a teeny giggle, because their order of elements fits in exactly with the three pillars and Malkuth (Figure 3).

At a recent science fiction convention, I participated in a panel on "Real Magic". Another panelist, author Jon deCles, pointed out that *The Dark Crystal* was a qabalistic

Fig 1

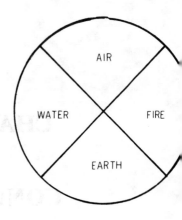

Fig 2

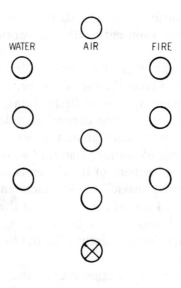

Fig 3

movie. The ten evil (but strong) skeksis represented the Pillar of Severity. The ten gentle (but ineffectual) mystics were the Pillar of Mercy.

"Unbalanced Mercy is weakness . . . Unbalanced Severity is cruelty . . . "

The Crystal itself was unholy because it was not complete, just as the Tree of Life would be unbalanced and incomplete if it lacked any one of its spheres.

When the skeksis and mystics (Vice and Virtues?) were rejoined and the missing shard replaced in the Crystal, balance (the Middle Pillar) was achieved and all was well.

Throughout life, through all phases of life, we go through the phases outlined in the Qabala, whether we study Qabala or not. The specific information dealing with energies, theology, thealogy and all aspects of the world beyond physical manifestation can be understood more clearly with the use of the Tree.

Using the symbological arrangement represented by the Tree is not a matter of forcing symbolism upon you, but a recognition and understanding of a pattern which already exists.

Joining this information to the joy and love found in the Craft of the Wise Ones, or any of the pagan philosophies, gives us a beautiful and effective way of spiritual growth. I, for one, would find Qabala and other ceremonial magic much too sombre without the other aspects of paganism. Without Qabala, I would not have the direction I have as a student and teacher.

In the following Appendices, I've organized the material discussed in previous chapters, and added further information. I encourage you to try them, use them, give this information a chance to enter your mind and heart. Let me share them with you.

Blessed be!

The Kingdom
Finds its Foundation
In Splendor and Victory.
Beauty is the balance
of Might and Mercy.
Understanding and Wisdom
Will lead me to the Crown.

APPENDIX I

THE SPHERES AND
THEIR CORRESPONDENCES

The information on the following pages includes: the Hebrew and English names of the sphere, a quote from the *Sefer Yetzirah* (The Book of Formation) as translated by Wynn Westcott, the Magical Image, the Name of Power, the Archangel, the Angels (Hebrew and English names), Planetary Attributions (Mundane Chakra), the Virtue, the Vice, Titles, Spiritual Experience, Deity Color, Archangel Color, Angel Color, Planetary Color, Symbols, Deities (examples of the Deities who can be placed in the sphere, but certainly not an exhaustive list), Precious Stones, the Plant, the Perfume, and the Animal.

MALKUTH–THE KINGDOM

"The Tenth Path is called the Resplendent Intelligence because it is exalted above every head and sits upon the Throne of Binah. It illuminates the splendors of all the lights and causes an influence to emanate from the Prince of Countenances, the Angel of Kether."

Magical Image:	A young woman, crowned and throned
Name of Power:	Adonai (Adonath) ha Aretz (Lord/ Lady of Earth), Adonai Malekh (Lord King)
Archangel:	Sandolphon
Angels:	Kerubim, the Strong
Planetary Attribution:	Earth, the planet
Virtue:	Discrimination
Vice:	Inertia
Titles:	The Gate. Kallah, the Bride, the Gate of Death. The Inferior Mother. The Gate of Justice. Malkah, the Queen. The Gate of Tears.
Spiritual Experience:	Vision of the Holy Guardian Angel
Deity Color:	Yellow
Archangel Color:	Ochre, Russet, Olive, Black
Angel Color:	Ochre, Russet, Olive, Black flecked with Gold
Planetary Color:	Black, rayed yellow
Symbols:	Altar of the Double Cube. The triangle of Art. The Equal Armed Cross. The Magic Circle.
Deities:	Earth and Grain Deities: Pan, Ceres, Demeter, Seb, Marduk,

Nisaba, Nerthus, Mati-Syra-Zem-
ba, Yorillo, Pellevvinen, Prith-
ivi, Tekketskerkok, Nokomis,
Ethinoha, Onathe, Chicomecoatl,
Niamh, Cernunnos, Myrddin

Precious Stones: Rock crystal
Plant: Willow, Lily, Ivy
Perfume: Dittany of Crete

YESOD—THE FOUNDATION

"The Ninth Path is called the Pure Intelligence because
it purifies the emanations. It proves and corrects the design-
of their representations, and disposes the unity with which
they are designed without diminuation or division."

Magical Image: A beautiful naked man, very
                            strong.
Name of Power: Shaddai El Chai, Almighty Living
                            One
Archangel: Gabriel
Angels: Aishim, the Souls of Fire
Planetary Attribution: The Moon
Virtue: Independence
Vice: Idleness
Titles: Treasurehouse of Images, the
                            Sphere of Illusion
Spiritual Experience: Vision of the Machinery of the
                            Universe
Deity Color: Indigo
Archangel Color: Violet
Angel Color: Very dark purple
Planetary Color: Citrine, flecked with azure

Symbols:	The perfumes and the sandals, the mirror
Deities:	All Moon Deities: Goda, Diana, Thoth, Ganesha, Hecate, Sin, Myestats, Kuu, Mah, Varuna, Soma, Ch'ango, Hengo, Tsuki-yomie, Pah, Coyolxauhqui, Quil-la, Auchimalgen
Precious Stones:	Quartz
Plant:	Mandrake, Banyan, Damiana
Animal:	Elephant, Tortoise, Toad
Perfume:	Jasmine, Ginseng, all fragrant roots

HOD—SPLENDOR, GLORY

"The Eighth Path is called the Absolute or Perfect Intelligence because it is the means of the Primordial, which hath no root by which it can cleave or rest, save in the hidden places of Gedulah, from which emanates its proper essence."

Magical Image:	An Hermaphrodite
Name of Power:	Elohim Tzabaoth (God/dess of Hosts)
Archangel:	Michael, Raphael
Angels:	Beni Elohim (Children of God/-dess)
Planet:	Mercury
Virtue:	Truthfulness
Vice:	Falsehood, Dishonesty
Spiritual Experience:	Vision of Splendor
Deity Color:	Violet Purple
Archangel Color:	Orange

Angel Color:	Russet Red
Planetary Color:	Yellowish black, flecked with white
Symbols:	Names, mantras, caduceus
Deities:	Messengers and Teachers: Thoth, Hermes, Mercury, Tautes, Ogma
Precious Stone:	Opal
Plant:	Moly
Perfume:	Storax (liquidambar gum)
Animal:	Jackal, twin serpents

NETZACH—VICTORY

"The Seventh Path is called the Occult Intelligence because it is the refulgent splendor of the intellectual virtues which are perceived by the eyes of the intellect and the contemplations of Faith.

Magical Image:	A beautiful naked woman
Name of Power:	Yahveh Tzabaoth (Lord of Hosts)
Archangel:	Haniel
Angels:	Elohim
Planetary Attribution:	Venus
Virtue:	Unselfishness
Vice:	Unchastity, Lust for Power
Titles:	Firmness, Valor, Eternity, Triumph
Spiritual Experience:	Vision of Beauty Triumphant
Deity Color:	Amber
Archangel Color:	Emerald
Angel Color:	Bright yellowish green
Planetary Color:	Olive, flecked with gold
Symbols:	Lamp, Girdle, the Rose
Deities:	All Love Deities: Venus, Ishtar, Aphrodite, Hathor, Rhiannon,

	Niamh, Cerridwen (for inspiration)
Precious Stone:	Emerald
Plant:	Rose
Perfume:	Rose, Benzoin, Red Sandalwood
Animal:	Lynx

TIFARETH—BEAUTY, HARMONY

"The Sixth Path is called the Mediating Intelligence because in it are multiplied the influxes of the emanations; for it causes that influence to flow into all reservoirs of the blessings with which they themselves are united.

Magical Image:	A king. A child. A sacrificed god.
Name of Power:	Yahveh Eloah Va Daath, God/-dess made Manifest in the Sphere of the Mind.
Archangel:	Raphael, Michael
Angels:	Malachim, Kings
Planetary Attribution:	The Sun
Virtue:	Devotion to the Great Work
Vice:	False Pride
Titles:	The Lesser Countenance
Spiritual Experience:	Vision of the Harmony of Things, Understanding the Mysteries of Sacrifice.
Deity Color:	Clear Rose Pink
Archangel Color:	Yellow
Angel Color:	Rich Salmon Pink
Planetary Color:	Golden Amber
Symbols:	The Red Cross, the Calvary Cross, the truncated pyramid, the lamen, the cube.

Deities:	Sun Deities, Holy Children, Healers, Sacrificed Gods, Illuminators: Osiris, Apollo, Attis, Adonis, Tammuz, Balder, Bran, Llew, Lugh, Gwern, Jesus, Dionysius, Balin, Ogma, Bride, Nonens, Shamash, Mot, Dozhbog, Parva, Huare-Khsaeta, Surya, Amaterasu, Koodjanuk, Shakuru, Tezcatlipoca, Inti, Apu, Panchai
Precious Stone:	Topaz, Yellow Diamond
Plant:	Acacia, Bay Laurel, Vine
Perfume:	Olibanum (frankincense)
Animal:	Phoenix, Lion

GEBURAH–MIGHT

"The Fifth Path is called the Radical Intelligence because it resembles Unity, uniting itself to Binah, Understanding, which emanates from the primordial depths of Chokmah, Wisdom."

Magical Image:	A mighty warrior in his/her chariot.
Name of Power:	Elohim Gibor, Mighty God/dess
Archangel:	Khamael
Angels:	Seraphim, Fiery Serpents
Planetary Attribution:	Mars
Virtue:	Energy, Courage
Vice:	Cruelty, Wanton Destruction
Titles:	Pachad, Fear; Din, Justice
Spiritual Experience:	Vision of Power
Deity Color:	Orange
Archangel Color:	Scarlet

Angel Color:	Bright Scarlet
Planetary Color:	Red, flecked with black
Symbols:	The Pentagon, the Sword, the Spear, the Scourge, the Chain, the Five-Petalled Tudor Rose.
Deities:	War, Protector, and Avenger Deities, Smith and Forge Deities: Mars, Ares, Bran, Minerva/Athena, Kali, the Morrigan, Lugh, Tubal Cain, Vulcan/Hephaestes, Ningurs, Culan, Odin, Vali, Pyrerun, Indra, Lei Kung, Okun-Nush, Huitzilopochtl
Precious Stone:	Ruby
Plant:	Oak, Nettle
Perfume:	Tobacco
Animal:	Basilisk

CHESED—MERCY

"The Fourth Path is called the Cohesive or Receptive Intelligence because it contains all the Holy Powers, and from it emanate all the spiritual virtues with the most exalted essences. They emanate one from another by virtue of the Primordial Emanation, the Highest Crown, Kether."

Magical Image:	A mighty crowned and throned king.
Name of Power:	El (God)
Archangel:	Tzadkiel
Angel:	Chasmalism, the Brilliant Ones
Planetary Attribution:	Jupiter
Virtue:	Obedience
Vice:	Bigotry, hypocrisy, gluttony

Titles:	Gedulah, Love, Majesty, Magnificence
Spiritual Experience:	Vision of Love
Deity Color:	Deep violet
Archangel Color:	Blue
Angel Color:	Deep Purple
Planetary Color:	Deep azure flecked yellow
Symbols:	The solid figure, Orb, Wand, the tetrahedron, Sceptre, Crook
Deities:	Benevolent Ruler Gods: Jupiter, Odin (as lawgiver) Nodens, etc.
Precious Stone:	Amethyst, Sapphire, Lapis Lazuli
Plant:	Olive, shamrock
Perfume:	Cedar
Animal:	Unicorn

BINAH—UNDERSTANDING

"The Third Path is called the Sanctifying Intelligence, the Foundation of Primordial Wisdom. It is also called the Creator of Faith and its roots are in Amen. It is the parent of faith from which faith emanates."

Magical Image:	A mature woman
Name of Power:	Yahveh Elohim
Archangel:	Tzafkiel
Angels:	Aralim, the Thrones
Planetary Attribution:	Saturn
Virtue:	Silence
Vice:	Avarice
Titles:	Ama, the dark sterile mother; Aima, the bright fertile mother; Marah, the Great Sea; Khorsia, the throne.

Spiritual Experience:	Vision of Sorrow
Deity Color:	Crimson
Archangel Color:	Black
Angel Color:	Dark brown
Planetary Color:	Grey flecked with pink
Symbols:	The Yoni, the cup or chalice
Deities:	Mother Goddesses, Saturnian Gods: Goda, Goide, Tautus (Tautatis), Olwen, Danu, Isis, Demeter, Tiamat, Kishar, Asherat, Gefjon, Parvati, Atira, Akna, Bran
Precious Stone:	Star Sapphire, Pearl
Plant:	Cypress, Lotus, Lily
Perfume:	Myrrh, Civet
Animal:	Bee

CHOKMAH—WISDOM

"The Second Path is called the Illuminating Intelligence. It is the Crown of Creation, the Splendor of unity, equalling it. It is exalted above every head and is named by Qabalists, the Second Glory.

Magical Image:	A bearded male figure
Name of Power:	Yahveh or Yah, Lord
Archangel:	Ratzkiel
Angels:	Auphanim, the Wheels
Planetary Attribution:	the Zodiac
Virtue:	Devotion
Vice:	—
Titles:	Power of Yetzirah, Ab, Abba, the Supernal Father
Spiritual Experience:	Vision of the Source We Seek

Deity Color:	Pure Soft Blue
Archangel Color:	Gray
Angel Color:	Pearl Gray, iridescent
Planetary Color:	White flecked with red, blue, yellow
Symbols:	The Phallus, Yod, the Tower, the straight line
Deities:	All Father Gods, God/desses of Wisdom, Priapic Gods: Zeus/-Jupiter, Great Pan, Osiris, the Dagda, Cernunnos, Tubal Cain, Nuada, (Nodens), Enki, Ashur, the Dagda, Ivarog, Izanagi, Tirawa, Udakanda
Precious Stone:	Star Ruby, Turquoise
Plant:	Amaranth
Perfume:	Musk
Animal:	Man

KETHER—THE CROWN

"The First Path is called the Admirable or Hidden Intelligence because it is the Light giving the power of comprehension of the First Principle, which hath no beginning. And it is the Primal Glory because no created being can attain to its essence."

Magical Image:	An ancient bearded king seen in profile.
Name of Power:	Eheieh, I am
Archangel:	Metatron
Angels:	Chioth ha Qadesh, Holy Living Creatures
Planetary Attribution:	First Swirlings

Virtue:	Attainment, Completion of the Great Work
Vice:	—
Titles:	Existence of Existences, Ancient of Days, the White Head, Macroprosopos, the Vast Countenance Lux Occulta (Hidden Light)
Spiritual Experience:	Reunion with the Source
Archangel Color:	Pure white brilliance
Planetary Color:	White flecked gold
Symbols:	The point, the swastika, the crown, point within a circle
Deities:	All Creator/Creatrix Deities: Ptah, Gaea, Jumala, Nipara, Nohochacyum, Ngai, Cagn
Precious Stones:	Diamond
Plant:	Flowering Almond
Perfume:	Ambergris
Animal:	The swan, the hawk

APPENDIX II

THE ASTRAL TEMPLES

THE TEMPLE OF MALKUTH

The floor is made up of black and white squares. In the center of the temple is a black altar, a double cube (one on top of the other) draped with a white cloth. On this altar you will find four candles in the colors of the elements, and the symbols of each element, each in its proper quadrant.

You can see pillars around the circumference of the temple, but cannot see beyond them to the walls.

To the East, you see two large pillars, a black one on the left, and a white one on the right.

Beyond and between the pillars you see a representation of the World Card of the Tarot, as large as a door. Above the card is a silver symbol of the Moon.

To the left of the black pillar, and beyond it, you see an equally large representation of the Judgment Card and above it, a symbol of Mercury.

To the right and beyond the white pillar, you see a door-sized representation of the Moon Card, surmounted by a symbol of Venus.

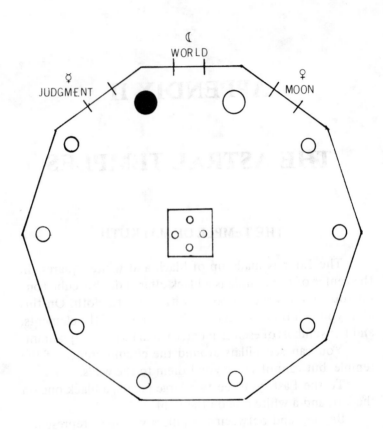

MALKUTH

Between the other pillars are statues of various gods and goddesses with small altars before them. If you wish to commune with one of them, you have only to go to the statue and meditate.

If you wish to meditate on the magical image, formulate it between the black and white pillars.

THE TEMPLE OF YESOD

The temple has nine sides and is made of quartz. In its center is a crescent-shaped altar, draped in violet. Behind the altar is a pedestal on which you can visualize the magical image, a beautiful naked man, if you desire to meditate on it.

The floor of the temple is of ever-changing shades of violet, lavender and purple.

Around the walls are altars to various moon dieties.

The temple has four doors, arranged as in the diagram. Each is represented by a Tarot card, and above each door is a planetary symbol.

The statues and altar trappings seem very elusive—their shapes and postures change as you watch.

More than any other sphere, your thoughts affect the appearance of this temple. If you do not see a statue representing the goddess you wish to adore, simply turn to an altar and picture her above it.

The doors out of the temple waver as well. Should you desire to exit through one of them, use the power of your mind to make the door firmly visible.

THE TEMPLE OF HOD

This temple has eight sides.

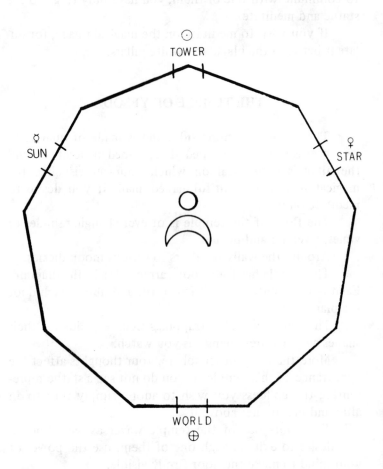

YESOD

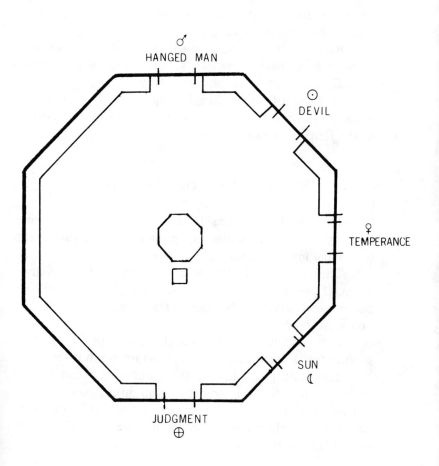

HOD

There are five doors, each a different Tarot card (see the diagram) and each with the symbol of a planet above it.

The altar is opal, with orange draperies. There is a fragrance of storax in the air.

Between the doors, filling shelves on every wall, are writings of some sort; books, scrolls, stone tablets, some incredibly ancient, some obviously new.

In front of the eight-sided opal altar is a pedestal. There you may form the magical image, or a representation of the Deity you wish to adore.

THE TEMPLE OF NETZACH

The temple has seven sides, although it has only narrow supports. It is surrounded by growing things, the green leaves making up the walls of this temple.

The seven-sided altar is a large emerald, clear and green. If you gaze into its depths, you will see there either the magical image of Netzach, or an image of the Deity you wish to adore.

Each of the five doors (in this case, openings in the greenery) is a Tarot card, with a planetary symbol above it.

The atmosphere here is the quiet of a forest glade, with the quiet broken only by small animal sounds and breezes rustling leaves. Yet you have the feeling of great energy here, hidden life flowing in the breeze, which carries with it the fragrance of roses.

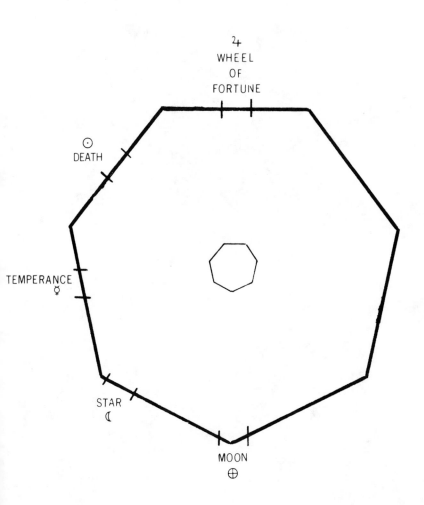

NETZACH

APPENDIX III

THE SPHERES
IN MAGICAL WORK

Whether you use the Qabalistic form of spell-casting, or any other method, you can use the Planetary Attributions of the spheres to define the sphere you wish to work with.

Work is almost never done with the energies of Kether and Chokmah, and Malkuth is the sphere of manifestation of everything, so this Appendix includes only the other seven spheres.

BINAH   Comfort in times of sorrow, help with groups, contact with the Goddess unveiled, development of the ability to listen and absorb.

CHESED   Expansion, growth, help from Ancient Ones, development of punctuality and neatness, (anything which deals with order) correction of stinginess, development of stability.

GEBURAH	Energy, courage, defense, getting rid of the unnecessary, vitality, development of will power and self-discipline.
TIFARETH	Honor, power, glory, life, growth, money, healing, illumination.
NETZACH	Love in all forms, pleasure, arts, music, creative energy, inspiration, help in overcoming lack of spontaneity, lack of emotion and lack of subjectivity. Breaking writer's block and similar problems.
HOD	Business, books, legal judgments, travel, information, the intellect, logic, writer's block (rather than needing inspiration, needing the ability to express your thought), helps curb over-emotionalism, helps organization of thoughts, develop learning skill, finding teachers and sources of information.
YESOD	Divination, change, understanding flux and reflux, fertility spells, development of intuition, better contact with unconscious, development of better memory.

APPENDIX IV

PRONUNCIATION GUIDE

The Hebrew found in this book, and others, is transliterated from the Hebrew alphabet to the alphabet we are familiar with. Most letters can be easily compared to ours, with two exceptions, the Hebrew "cheth" and "tav".

"Cheth" in this volume is represented by the letters "ch", and is pronounced almost as a clearing of the throat, a guttural sound as found in the Scottish pronunciation of the word "loch". If you are not sure of the sound, ask a Jewish friend to pronounce "chutzpah".

"Tav" is, in this book, represented by the letters "th", but they do not represent the "th-" sound found in such English words as "the" or "thin". "Tav" represents a very breathy "t". "Kether" for example, is pronounced "Kether".

E — as in bet
A — as in father
I — as in bit
O — boat
U — boot

In the word "Tzabaoth" the "a" after the "b" represents a glottal stop rather than a sound. A glottal stop is the tightening of the throat that makes the difference between the sound of "a nice man" and "an ice man". The word could also be written "Tzab'oth", which might be clearer.

As for knowing which syllable to accent, most Hebrew words are accented on the last or next to last syllable. The following words are examples:

> KE — ter
> Chok — MAH
> Bin — AH
> CHE — sed
> Gebur — AH (the "b" in Hebrew is very soft—almost a "v")
> Ti — FAR — eth
> Net — ZACH
> Ye — SOD
> Mal — KUTH
> Elo — HIM
> Da — ATH

APPENDIX V

THE SHARED CROSS

This is a form of the Qabalistic cross that is, as the name implies, shared by more than one person. It can be used at any time a sharing is appropriate, a handfasting, for example.

In its most basic form, it is performed thusly:

The two persons join both hands, and one of them speaks as they visualize a ball of light above and between them.

"May we share always the light of the Goddess"
The light is seen to come down between them, touching both to their feet.

"The wisdom to be gained in her kingdom"
The light is seen crossing between and touching them, from the speaker's right shoulder to the left.

"Her strength, her mercy and her love"
At the words "her love" a sphere of light is seen at the center of the cross, and as the following words, the sphere grows until it encompasses both persons.

Fig 1   Fig 2   Fig 3

CIRCLE SHARED CROSS

Fig 4

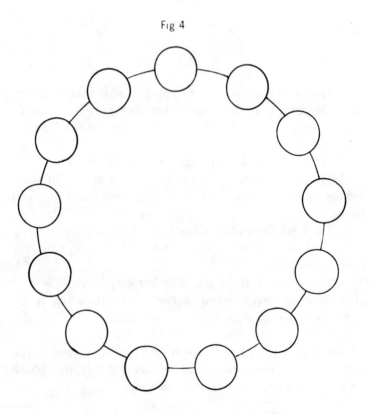

"Which is manifest in our love for each other"
The two may stand as long as they like in that circle of loving light.

The Alternate Shared Cross

This is performed in the same way except that the persons alternate in speaking the words:

A: May we share always the light of the Goddess
B: The wisdom to be gained in her kingdom
A: Her strength
B: Her mercy
A: And her love
B: Which is manifest in our love for each other

Circle Shared Cross

This is a lovely way to greet a new member into a group.

1. The Shared Cross is performed by two persons. When it is done, one of the persons steps away toward the next in the circle. (Fig. 1)

2. As the two persons part, the sphere of light which surrounds them divides so that each remain in a sphere of light, the two spheres connect by a "cord" of light. (Fig. 2)

3. The Shared Cross is performed with the next person in the circle. During this, when the sphere of light is formed in the center of the cross, it is even more brilliant than the light already there, and when this sphere is expanded, it is brighter still. This added brilliance can be seen also in the cord joining the sphere of the original person shared with.

4. As the person circling steps away from the second person, the sphere again divides. (Fig. 3)

5. This continues around the circle, with the light becoming more and more brilliant as the energies

of each person are added to it.

6.   When the circle is completed, the circling person joins
      hands with the first, joining their spheres, then sepa-
      rating to form the cord of light, making a complete
      circle of light, studded with brilliant spheres, like a
      necklace of the Goddess. (Fig. 4)

APPENDIX VI

THE RITE OF MENDING LOVE

This ritual is to be used when the dissension between two of its members is such that a circle is threatened. It must, obviously, be entered into freely by the two persons involved.

While most of the ritual is performed by the two quarrelling members, presided over by the High Priest or High Priestess, the other members of the circle should add their energies to each step.

It must be kept in mind by all, especially the two quarrelling members, that during the lighting of the orange, green and yellow candles, each speaks for both. When one says "Let unreasoning anger be blown away", they are *both* saying it.

While the Goddess name used is Isis, you may use the name normally used by your coven, or simply "Lady".

Where the instructions read "HP/S" it is left to your discretion whether the High Priestess or High Priest speaks, or if the words are shared by both.

ALTAR
ARRANGEMENT

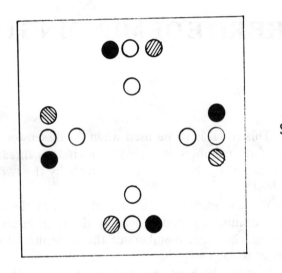

 ORANGE

○ YELLOW

● GREEN

A central altar should be set up per the diagram, with four candles at each quadrant: the three nearest the edge symbolizing the spheres of Hod, Tifareth and Netzach.

The single candle placed nearer the center represents the element of that quadrant. My tradition uses yellow for Air, red for Fire, blue for Water and green for Earth. You should, of course, follow the attributions of your own tradition.

If, as is the case with Air and Earth in my tradition, some elemental colors match the Qabalistic colors, you should use different shades of that color. For example, a bright emerald for Netzach and a forest green for Earth.

Nearby should be kept two violet 7-day candles in glass, healing oil and a work knife.

The method of circle casting is left to you.

CIRCLE IS CAST

HP/P   Hail, Isis, Mother of us all. We do ask your help in this our time of need. Two of your children find it impossible to resolve their differences without your help. They come before you to ask your guidance in their trouble, knowing that by their dissension they weaken not only themselves, but the circle as well.

The two Quarrelling Members (hereafter referred to as QM1 and QM2) come forward to stand behind HP/S. HP/S turns to face them.

HP/S   An incomplete circle is not a circle. Without fellowship, without love among *all* its sisters and brothers, this circle cannot be complete. Therefore, let us banish all anger, all argument between you, with the help of the gods.

QM1   Isis, my Mother, I _____ do ask your help in banishing the dissension between my brother/sister, _____ _____, and me.

QM2   (repeats above)

All three go to center altar, at the east side, facing west.

HP/S   Mercury, Hermes, Thoth, all ye Gods of Hod, Gods of Reason and Communication, hear me. Let your powers of logic and reason enter these children of the Goddess, circle them that they may use these powers in their dealings with each other.

At each quadrant, QM1 lights candle from proper elemental candle, speaks, then hands candle to QM2 who touches candle again to elemental candle, speaks and replaces the candle on the altar.

QM1   Let unreasoning anger be blown away.

QM2   And replace it with sensibility and logic.

TO THE SOUTH

QM1   Let angry words without meaning burn away

QM2   And be replaced with the light of true communication.

TO THE WEST

QM1   Let all misunderstandings be washed from memory.

QM2   And leave only those moments of true sharing.

TO THE NORTH

QM1   Let the wall we have built between us crumble.

QM2   And become a smooth road we may walk together.

Return to the East.

HP/S   Venus, Aphrodite, Rhiannon, ye Goddesses of Net-Zach, goddesses of love in all forms, hear me. Let your powers of love, of caring, of joy, enter these children of the Goddess, circle them that they may use these powers in their dealings with each other.

TO THE EAST

QM1   Let the air between us contain only love.

QM2   And the winds of change bring a stronger friendship.

TO THE SOUTH

QM1   Let the powers of fire bring warmth to our relationship.

QM2   And the light of love banish the darkness of anger.

TO THE WEST

QM1   Let the power of water clean our friendship of its past harmful influences.

QM2   And heal the wounds we've given each other.

TO THE NORTH

QM1   Let the powers of Earth strengthen our love for each other.

QM2   That we may strengthen each other with that love.

Return to the East.

HP/S   Gods of Tifareth, Gods of Beauty and Harmony, hear me. Let your powers of balance, of re-birth enter these children of the Goddess, circle them that they may use these powers in their dealings with each other.

TO THE EAST

QM1   The winds have blown away the imbalancing forces against us.

QM1   Let us share the cool and pleasant breezes.

TO THE SOUTH

QM1   The fires have burned away our anger.

QM2   Let us share the warmth and light of the Sun.

TO THE WEST

QM1   The rains have washed away the sorrows we've given each other.

QM2   Let us share the soothing wounds of the waves.

TO THE NORTH

QM1   We have planted the seeds of friendship in the fertile earth.

QM2   Let us share the work of tending it, and the pleasure in its growing.

The two return to the East, take up the purple candles. Each dresses one, and marks it with whatever symbolism is meaningful to them, sharing the oil and knife to do so.

When the candles are prepared, they are lighted. QM1 presents candle toward the Goddess, asking a blessing, then turns to QM2 holding out candle. QM2 places hands on candle and they both hold it as QM1 speaks:

QM1   This candle, in a color sacred to the Goddess, is a symbol of my love for Her, and therefore my love for you. As it burns, let it also burn away those astral beings that represent anything other than the friendship and love I feel for you. As this candle grows smaller, so does any chance of misunderstanding. As the space above it grows larger, so does the strength of the bond between us. Will you accept this candle and its meanings, giving in return your forgiveness for my thoughtlessness and foolishness?

QM2   I will, gladly, and with a whole heart.

Candle is placed on altar. QM2 presents the candle he has prepared for a blessing, then presents it to QM1, repeating the above, and receiving the same answer.

QM1 and Qm2 turn to each other, join hands and perform the Alternate Shared Cross. They should stand so as long as they feel necessary. At this point, they may add anything they feel appropriate, such as an exchange of gifts, or whatever words come to mind. They then return to their original places in the circle.

HP/S   Once again we are a complete circle.

Group join hands

HP/S   Once again the energies pass from one to the other, ever-growing in strength and skill. We are an unbroken chain, each link complete within itself, and each link joined to the other. Our circle is whole again. Let us rejoice in our hearts for our brother/sister _____ and our brother/sister _____ .

CLOSE CIRCLE

RECOMMENDED READING

The following books are only a few of those available. Others will be found in the bibliography. The books on this list, however, will give you as complete an understanding of the mystical Qabala as any teaching method can. Qabala, more than any other subject, is best learned through study and meditation. Just as teachers cannot *teach* the Mysteries, any book, however excellent, cannot *teach* you Qabala, but rather lead you toward an understanding of its Mysteries. The personal work you do, the amount of effort you are willing to put forth control the amount to be gained.

These authors do not always agree with each other, nor will you (nor do I). Don't let any of the comments made by the authors keep you from learning from them. They each have much to share with you, if you will be open-minded to receive it. Some of them reflect prejudices against homosexuals, and some against witches. (One of them defended his comments on the subject by reminding me that his book was written before the true information was widely available about the Craft. He promises not to do it anymore.) In spite of the Qabala's recognition of the Goddess, many of the books are extremely God-oriented. Don't be foolish. These authors are sharing years of experience and work with you. Let them share it.

The Mystical Qabala, by Dion Fortune
   One of the best books to be found on Qabala. It will give you a superb basic knowledge to work with.
Ladder of Lights, by W. G. Gray
   Its arrangement and presentation of the material is very different from most books on Qabala. It concentrates on the Four Worlds of each sphere and is of immeasurable value in developing your understanding of them.
A Practical Guide to Qabalistic Symbolism, Vol I, by Gareth Knight
   This book contains enough suggestions for meditations to keep you busy for years. The other information is as helpful. Gareth Knight is a Christian Qabalist, and many of his references are from the Christian mythos. This can be helpful to those with a Christian background, but distracting to those without. It would be a shame to miss the information in this book because you lack tolerance for another faith.

Occult Psychology, by A. LaDage

With or without a psychological background, you will gain a lot from this interface of Qabala with Jungian psychology.

An Introduction to the Mystical Qabala, by Alan Richardson

This little book is especially helpful in applying Qabala to your magical work.

The Sword and the Serpent, by Denning and Phillips

This book is the result of study and experience by a modern magical lodge and offers yet another point of view. For example, they present alternate color scales you might prefer to the "traditional". *The Sword and the Serpent* is one of a series of *The Magical Philosophy*.

The Tree of Life, by Israel Regardie

Along with information on the Qabala, this will introduce you to other aspects of ceremonial magic and its ideologies you may find useful. If you wish to learn more about the Paths between the spheres, these two books are valuable.

Practical Guide to Qabalistic Symbolism, Vol 2, by Gareth Knight

To my knowledge, this is one of only two books which dwell on the paths with any detail at all. The information to be gained by working on each path is included, as well as various correspondences. Both volumes of this work will appeal to those of you who are artists, for they contain descriptions that cry to be painted.

The Living Tree, by W. G. Gray

Mr. Gray has, as always, chosen his own individual way of expressing himself. It is a very interesting book.

With few exceptions, all of these books have been with me since I first began to study Qabala, and I've read each of them many times.

When I began to teach Qabala, I re-read all of them. During the preparation of my lecture, I read them yet again. This book required at least one more reading.

Each time certain phrases leaped to my eye, certain sentences and paragraphs were especially meaningful. The amazing thing was, they were never the same phrases or paragraphs. The "purple patches" were, each time, those which related to my status with each reading: student, teacher, lecturer, writer.

Even in written form, the Qabala is wondrous!

BIBLIOGRAPHY

Butler, W.E., *Magic and the Qabala*. Aquarian Press, London, Eng., 1964.

Crowley, A., *777*. Samuel Weiser, New York, NY, 1970.

Denning, Melita, and Phillips, Osborne, *Sword and the Serpent*. Llewellyn, St. Paul, MN, 1975.

Donavon, Frank, *Never On A Broomstick*. Stackpole Books, Harrisburg, PA, 1971.

Fortune, Dion, *The Mystical Qabalah*. Samuel Weiser, New York, NY, 1984.

Frazer, Sir James, *The Golden Bough*. McMillan Pub., New York, NY, 1974.

Frank, Adolph, *The Kabbalah*. University Books, Secaucus, NJ, 1967.

Graves, Robert, *The White Goddess*. Faber and Faber, Winchester, MA, 1947.

Gray, W.G., *Ladder of Lights*. Helios Book Service, Ltd. Great Britain, 1968.

Hall, Manly P., *Cabalistic Keys to the Lord's Prayer*. Philosophical Research Soc., Los Angeles, CA, 1964.

Hawkridge, Emma, *The Wisdom Tree*. Houghton Mifflin, Boston, MA, 1945.

Knight, Gareth, *Practical Guide to Qabalistic Symbolism*. Helios Book Service Pub., Great Britain, 1965.

LaDage, Alta, *Occult Psychology*. Llewellyn, St. Paul, MN, 1978.

LaRousse, *Encyclopedia of Mythology*.

Levi, Eliphas, *The Book of Splendours*. Weiser, New York, NY. 1973.

Moody, Raymond, *Life After Life*. Bantam Books, New York, NY, 1976.

Ponce, Charles, *Kabbalah*. Theos. Pub. House, Wheaton, IL, 1978.

Game of Wizards.

Regardie, Israel, *Art of True Healing*. Helios, Great Britain, 1974.

Garden of Pomegranates. Llewellyn, St. Paul, MN, 1974.

Golden Dawn. Llewellyn, St. Paul, MN, 1982.

Middle Pillar. Llewellyn, St. Paul, MN, 1970.

The Tree of Life. Weiser, New York, NY, 1983.

Richardson, Alan, *Introduction to the Mystical Qabala*. Weiser, New York, NY, 1974.

Schaya, L., *Universal Meaning of the Kabbalah*, University Books, Secaucus, NJ, 1971.

Seven Pupils of E.G., *Mysteries of the Qabalah*. Yogi Publication Soc., Chicago, IL, 1922.

Sinclair, David, *Drum and Candle*. Doubleday and Co., Garden City, NY, 1971.

Starhawk, *Spiral Dance*. Harper and Row, San Francisco,

Von Rosenroth, Knorr, *Aesch Mexareph*. Occult Research Press, New York, NY.

Westcott, Wynn, *Sepher Yetzirah*. Weiser, New York, NY, 1976.

INDEX

Ab: 124
Abba: 124
Acacia: 121
Achievement: 50
Adam and Eve: 74
Adepts: 33
Adeptus Exemptus: 34, 35
Adeptus Minor: 48
Adonai: 21
Adonai Ha Aretz: 74, 115
Adonai Malekh: 115
Adonath: 74, 115
Adonis: 47, 121
Aima: 30, 123
Ain Soph: 17, 18, 20, 27, 109
Ain Soph Aur: 17
Air: 74, 103, 145
Air Grade: 103
Aishim: 64, 66, 117
Akasha: 63
Akashic Records: 29
Akna: 124
Almond, Flowering: 126
Altar of the Double Cube: 115
Ama: 30, 123
Amaranth: 125
Amaterasu: 47, 121
Amergris: 126
Amethyst: 123
Amoun: 33
Ancient of Days: 126
Ancient Ones: 34
Angels: 2, 29, 36, 51, 60, 64, 66, 73, 114
Animal: 114
Aphrodite: 51, 119, 146
Apollo: 47, 121
Approacher: 73
Apu: 121
Aralim: 29, 123
Arcana, Major: 94
Arcana, Minor: 94
Archangel: 19, 23, 29, 36, 49, 65, 73, 77, 83, 91, 93, 114
Archangels: 14
Archetypal Temple: 29
Archetypal World: 77
Ares: 41, 122
art therapy: 54, 60
Arthur, King: 43, 37
Ascended Masters: 34

Asherat: 124
Ashur: 125
Assiah: 77, 79
Astral: 63
Astral temples: 90, 108, 127
Athena: 41, 122
Atira: 124
Attainment: 20, 126
Attis: 121
Atziluth: 77, 90
Auchimalgen: 118
Auphanim: 23, 124
Auriel: 74
Autumn: 79
Avarice: 30, 123
Avenger Deities: 122

Bach, Richard: 17
barbarous names of evocation: 11
Balder: 47, 121
Balin: 121
Banyan: 118
Basilik: 122
Bay Laurel: 121
Beauty: 45, 53, 120, 147
Bee: 124
Beni Elohim: 59, 118
Big Bang: 20
bigotry: 36, 122
Binah-Chapter Five: 27-31, 60, 66, 69, 72, 73, 83, 84, 94, 100, 115, 121, 123, 134
Blavatsky, Madame: 1
books: 57, 58, 60, 132
books, occult: 60
Brahma: 19
Bran: 28, 42, 121, 122, 124
Branwen: 2
Briah: 77
Bride: 121
Buddha: 47
Bull: 19
Butler, W.E.: 3, 84
Caduceus: 119
Cain: 125
cauldron: 30
Cauldron of Cerridwen: 28
Cedar: 123
Celtic Deities: 12

Ceres: 72, 115
Cernunnos: 117, 125
Cerridwen: 28, 120 (for inspiration)
Chain: 122
Chalice: 123
Ch'ango: 118
Chasmalim: 36, 122
Chesed-Chapter Six: 33-36, 39, 41, 43, 44, 118, 122, 124
Chicomecoatl: 117
child: 120
children: 121
Chioth ha Qadesh: 125
Chokmah-Chapter Four: 21-25, 31, 60, 83, 94, 100, 121, 124, 134
Christian(ity): 2, 35, 48
Civet: 124
Completion of the Great Work: 126
correspondence: 76
Cosmic Egg: 20
Countenance, Greater: 45
Countenance, Lesser: 45, 120
Countenance, Vast: 126
Courage: 121
Craft: 12, 35, 37, 40, 67, 73, 103, 113
Craft of the Wise Ones: 2
Creation, World of: 77
Creator/Creatrix: 19, 126
Crone: 30, 63
Cronos: 19
crook: 39, 123
Cross, Calvary: 120
Cross, Equal-armed: 115
Cross, Qabalistic: 87
Cross, Red: 120
Cross, Shared: 137
Cross, Alternate Shared: 141
Cross, Circle Shared: 141
Crowley: 84, 94
Crown: 17, 73, 124, 125, 126
Cruelty: 121
cryptograms: 57
cube: 120
Culan: 120
cup: 123
Cypress: 124

Dagda: 2, 125
Damiana: 118

Danu: 29, 124
Dark Crystal: 111
death: 48
Death: 47
deCles, Jon: 111
Degrees (Craft), First: 101, 107
Degrees, Second: 48
Deities: 114
Deities, Healing: 47
Deities, Illuminators: 47
Deity Name: 10
Demeter: 28, 29, 115, 124
Destruction: 39
Destruction, Wanton: 121
Devotion: 25, 124
Devotion to the Great Work: 49, 120
Diamond: 126
Diamond, yellow: 121
Diana: 118
Din: 37, 121
Dionysus: 47, 121
Discrimination: 75, 115
Dishonesty: 57, 104, 118
Dittany of Crete: 75, 76, 117
Dius Pitar: 24
Douglas, Lloyd C.: 68
Doshbog: 121
drugs: 58

Eagle: 19
earth: 72
Earth: 41, 72, 74, 115, 145
Earth Grade: 103
Eater of Hearts: 66
Eden: 74
Ehieh: 19, 125
El: 36, 122
Elements: 73, 77, 106
Elephants: 118
Eloah: 30
Elohim: 30, 119
Elohim (angels) 51, 59
Elohim Gibor: 43, 121
Elohim Tzabaoth: 118
Emerald: 120
Emperor: 94
Energy: 121
Enki: 125
E Pluribus Unum: 53
Eternity: 119

Existence of Existences: 126

Falsehood: 57, 118
False Pride: 49, 120
Father, Great: 21, 125
Father, Heavenly: 2
Father, Supernal: 124
Fear: 121, 145
Fiery Serpents: 43, 121
Fire: 74
Fire Grade: 106
First Swirlings: 17, 125
flail: 39
Flashing Colors: 77
Forge (Deities): 122
Formation, World of: 77
Fortune, Dion: 3, 84
Foundation: 63
Four Worlds: 1, 14, Chapter 13 (77-80), 83
Frigga: 28
Furies: 43

Gabriel: 65, 66, 75, 117
Gaea: 19, 126
Ganesha: 118
Geburah-Chapter Seven: 37-44, 28, 36, 58, 83, 88, 106, 111, 121, 136
Gedulah: 33, 88, 94, 118, 124
gematria: 16
Ghandi: 47, 48
Girdle: 119
Givers of Illumination: 47
Glory: 57, 118, 124, 125
gluttony: 36, 122
Goda: 118, 124
Goide: 124
Golden Dawn: 43
Goddesses, Avenger: 122
Goddesses, Creatrix, 19, 125
Goddesses, Great Mother: 28, 124
Goddesses, Protector: 122
Goddesses, Triple: 63
Goddesses, Underworld: 29
Goddesses, Wisdom: 125
Gods: 48
Gods, Avenger: 122
Gods, Creator: 19, 126
Gods, Great Father: 24, 124

Gods, Forge: 42
Gods, Messenger: 57
Gods, Priapic: 24, 125
Gods, Protector: 122
Gods, Smith: 42
Gods, Teaching: 57
Gods, Underworld: 28
Gods, War: 41
Gods, Wisdom: 125
Grace: 33
Grahame, Kenneth: 39
Grand Canyon: 40
Grant, Joan: 99
Graves, Robert: 53
Gray, W.G.: 2, 65
Greater Countenance: 45
Great Father: 21, 31, 125
Great Father Gods: 24
Great God Pan: 24, 125
Great Mother: 28, 31
Great Mother Goddesses: 28
Greatness: 33
Great Rite: 61
Great Sea: 123
Great Work: 20, 74, 125
Greed: 30
Green Light: 68
grimoires: 60
Gwern: 47, 121

Hall of Judgment: 42
Hall of Karma: 42
Hall of the Masters: 34
Haniel: 51, 119
Harmony: 45, 53, 120, 147
Hathor: 51, 119
Hawk: 126
Healer (deities): 121
Hecate: 118
Hengo: 118
Hephaestes: 42, 122
Hermaphrodite: 59, 60, 118
Hermes: 145
High Priest: 49, 106, 109, 145
High Priestess: 49, 109, 143
Hod: 53, 55, Chapter 10 (57-62), 83, 94, 100, 104, 108, 118
Holy Living Creatures: 19, 125
Horus: 47
Huare-Khasata: 121

Huitzilophoctl: 121
humility: 49, 50
hypocrisy: 36, 122
Idleness: 66, 103, 117
Illuminators: 121
Illusion, Sphere of: 99, 117
Impurity: 54
Incense: 76
Indra: 33
Independence: 117
Inertia: 74, 96, 99, 103, 115
Intelligence: 27
Intelligence, Absolute: 118
Intelligence, Admirable: 125
Intelligence, Cohesive: 122
Intelligence, Hidden: 125
Intelligence, Mediating: 120
Intelligence, Occult: 119
Intelligence, Perfect: 118
Intelligence, Pure: 117
Intelligence, Radical: 121
Intelligence, Receptive: 122
Intelligence, Resplendent: 72, 115
Intelligence, Sanctifying: 123
Inti: 121
Isis: 28, 29, 124, 143, 145
Isis-Urania: 24
Ivarog: 125
Ivy: 117
Iznagi: 125

Jackal: 119
Jasmine: 118
Jehovah: 21, 23
Jesus: 47, 48, 121
JHVH: 21, 23, 94
Joshua: 5
Justice: 121
Judaism: 4, 21, 48
Judges: 5
Judgment: 37
Jung, Carl Gustave: 1
Jupiter: 24, 33, 123, 125
Jupiter, planet: 33, 122

Kabbalah: 4
Kali: 42
Karma: 42
Karma, Hall of: 42
Kerubim: 65

Kether, Chapter 3: (17-20), 21, 45,
    122, 125, 135
Khamael: 43, 59, 121
Khorsia: 29
king: 71
King Arthur: 43, 47
King, Martin Luther: 47
King, Sun: 48
kingdom: 71, 76, 88
Kishar: 124
Knight, Gareth: 3, 84, 90
Koodhanuk: 121
Krishna: 47
Kung Fu: 30
Kuu: 118
Kwan Shi Yin: 24
Kwan Yin: 28

LaDage, A.: 2
Lamen: 120
Lamp: 119
Lapis Lazuli: 124
laser: 16
Lei Kung: 122
Lesser Countenance: 45
Lily: 117, 124
Lion: 19, 121
Llew: 47, 121
London Fire: 40
Lotus: 124
Love: 88
Love Deities: 119
Lugh: 47, 121
Lux Occulta: 125

Macroporsopos: 125
Magical Circle: 76, 116
Magical image: 11, 25, 30, 34, 39,
    49, 59, 69, 72, 107, 114
Magical Work: 92
Magic, black: 15
Magic, instinctive: 60
Magic, natural: 60
Magic, ritual: 61
Magnificence: 123
Mah: 118
Maiden: 57
Majesty: 122
Malachim: 120
Malkah: 115

Malkuth: 63, 65, 66, 69, 83, 84, 90, 93, 96, 97, 100, 103, 109, 111, 115, 127, 134
Man: 19, 125
Mandrake: 118
Manifestation, World of: 77
mantras: 60, 91, 108, 119
Marah: 31, 123
Marduk: 115
Mars: 41, 122
Mars (planet): 33, 121
Mary: 29
Mati-Sura-Zemba: 117
Maya: 28
Meditation: 31, 89
Meditation, Group: 108
Mercury: 119, 145
Mercury (planet): 57, 118, 127
Mercy: 33, 45, 88, 122
Messenger (deities): 119
Metatron: 19, 125
Michael: 49, 58, 74, 118, 120
Might: 37, 121
Minerva: 41, 122
Mirror: 64, 118
Moly: 119
Moon: 63, 64, 91, 110, 117, 127
Moon Deities: 117
Moon Rite: 108
Morrigan: 122
Moses: 5
Moses de Leon: 5
Mot: 121
Mother: 30, 63
Mother, Heavenly: 2
Mother, Goddesses: 124
Mother, Inferior: 115
Mother, bright fertile: 30, 123
Mother, dark sterile: 30, 123
Mother, Nature: 41
Mount St. Helen: 36
mundane chakras: 11, 79, 114
muse: 53
Musk: 125
Myestats: 118
Myrddin: 117
Mysteries: 13, 107
Mysteries, Egyptian: 5
Mysteries, Received teachings: 4

Name: 119
Name of Power: 10, 21, 30, 53, 64, 74, 93, 115
Names of Power: 4
Nature: 61
Neophyte, Grade: 100
Neophyte, ritual: 43
Nerthus: 117
Nettle: 122
Netzach-Chapter 9: (51-55), 59, 60, 69, 83, 106, 111, 117, 132, 136, 145
Ngai: 126
Niamh: 117, 119
Ningurs: 122
Nipara: 126
Nisabe: 117
Nohochacyum: 125
Nokomia: 117
Nodens: 126
Nonens: 121
Notaricon: 16
Nuada: 125

Oak: 122
Obedience: 35, 122
Odin: 24, 122, 123
Ogma: 119
Old Testament: 74
Olibaum: 121
Olive: 123
Olorun: 24
Olwen: 124
Onanthe: 117
Opal: 119, 132
Osiris: 33, 34, 47, 66, 119, 125
Ox: 19

Pachad: 37, 39
pagan(s): 10, 33, 48, 80
Paganism: 4
Pagan Mythology: 12, 51
Pah: 118
Pan: 24, 39, 125
Panchai: 121
Parva: 121
Parvati: 124
Path, 32nd: 71, 108
Path, Tenth: 115
Path, Ninth: 117

Path, Eighth: 118
Path, Seventh: 119
Path, Sixth: 120
Path, Fifth: 121
Path, Fourth: 122
Path, Third: 123
Path, Second: 124
Path, First: 125
Pearl: 124
Pellevvinen: 115
Penis: 24
pentagon: 43, 122
pentagram: 60
Perfect Love: 35
perfume: 75, 115
Perfumes: 13
Persephone: 29
Personality(ies): 66, 74, 106
Phallus: 125
Pharaoh: 39
Philosophy, Eastern: 1, 67
Philosophy, Oriental: 2
Philosophy, Western: 2, 67
Phoenix: 50, 121
pillars: 7
Pillar, black/white: 127, 128
Pillar, Feminine: 7, 29, 59, 60
Pillar, Masculine: 7, 21, 49, 53, 59
Pillar, Middle: 7, 103, 113
Pillar of Balance: 10
Pillar of Equilibrium: 7
Pillar of Expansion: 10, 29
Pillar of Force: 10, 29, 53, 111, 113
Pillar of Form: 10
Pillar of Mercy: 7
Pillar of Mildness: 7
Pillar of Restriction: 10, 111
Pillar of Severity: 113
Planetary attribution: 5, 11, 29, 45,
    51, 57, 114, 134
plant: 14, 114
Pluto: 66
Point: 125
"Pompous Ass" stage: 107
prayer: 31
Pre-Christian religions: 3
Precious Stones: 14, 114
Pride: 49
Pride, False: 107
Primum Mobile: 17

Prithvi: 117
Prophet: 30
Protector (deities): 122
psychiatry: 1
Psychology: 1
Ptah: 19
puns: 60
puzzles: 60
Pyrerun: 122
Pyramid, truncated: 120

Qabala, definition: 2
Qabala, mystical, 4, 5, 26
Qabala, origin: 5
Qabala, spelling: 4
Qabalah: 4
Qabalism: 3
Quartz: 118
Quilla: 118

Ra: 47
radar: 16
Rama: 47
Raphael: 49, 58, 74, 118, 120
Ratzkiel: 23
Rebirth: 47
Regardie, Israel: 3, 84
Reunion with the Source: 20, 15
Rhiannon: 51, 119, 145
Rising on the Planes: 90, 93
ritual: 57, 60, 61, 109
rock crystal: 117
Romans: 41
roots: 118
Rose: 119
Rose, Tudor: 122
Ruby: 122
Ruby, Star: 125

Sacred Children: 47
sacrifice: 48
Sacrificed Gods: 121
Sacrificed Kings: 47
St. Paul: 12
Sakti: 28
sandals: 118
Sandalwood: 120
Sandolphon: 73
Saturn: 28
Saturn (planet): 28, 33, 123

Saturnian God: 124
Sceptre: 123
Scourge: 122
Scrolls: 132
Seb: 72, 115
Sefer Yetzirah: 14, 72, 114
sephiroth: 7
Seraphim: 43
Serpents, Fiery: 43, 121
serpents, twin: 119
Severity: 45
Shaddai El Chai: 64, 117
Shakespeare: 59
Shakuru: 121
Shamash: 121
Shamrock: 123
Silence: 31, 123
Sin: 118
Sinai: 5
Smith (deities): 122
Soma: 118
Source: 75
Spiritual Experience: 12, 23, 28, 34,
    47, 53, 59, 68, 74, 114
Splendor: 118
Spring: 79
Star: 94
Stone tablets: 132
Storax: 110, 132
Strength: 88
Summer: 79
Summerland: 66
Sun: 45, 47, 57, 120
Sun Deities: 121
Surya: 121
Swan: 126
Swastika: 126
sword: 65, 122
Symbols: 114

Tai Chi'n: 31
Tarot: 5, 65, 94
Tarot Card, Emperor: 94
Tarot Card, Judgment: 127
Tarot Card, Moon: 127
Tarot Card, Star: 94
Tarot Card, World: 127
Tautatis: 124
Tautis: 124
Teachers (deities): 119

Tekketskerkok: 117
telesmic images: 59
Temple, Archetypal: 28
temples, astral: 90, 108
Temple of Hod: 91, 127, 129
Temple of Malkuth: 91, 127
Temple of Netzach: 91, 131
Temple of Yesod: 91, 129
Temura: 16
tetrahedron: 123
Tezcatlipoca: 121
Theosophists: 1
Thoth: 92, 118, 119, 145
thoughtform: 59
throne: 23, 29, 73, 123
Thrones: 23, 29
Tiamat: 124
Tifareth-Chapter 8: (45-50), 83, 93,
    100, 110, 111, 120, 135, 145,
    147
Tirawa: 125
Titles: 114
Toad: 118
Tobacco: 121
Tolkien: 97
Topaz: 121
Tortoise: 118
Tower: 125
Treasurehouse of Images: 64, 66,
    117
Tree of Evil: 15
Tree of Life: 4, 7, 11, 13, 25, 41,
    81, 87, 109, 113
Triangle of Art: 76, 115
Triumph: 119
Truthfulness: 58, 104, 118
Tubal-Cain: 42, 122
Turquoise: 125
Twain, Mark: 105
twin serpents: 119
Tzaddi: 94
Tzadkiel: 30, 122
Tzafkiel: 29, 123
Unchastity: 119
Udakanda: 125
Understanding: 27, 123
Understanding of Perfect Love: 34
Understanding the Mysteries of the
    Crucifixion: 48
Understanding the Mysteries of

Sacrifice: 48, 120
Underworld: 66
Underworld God/desses: 28
Unicorn: 36, 123
Union with God: 20
Unselfishness: 54, 119

Vali: 122
Valor: 119
Varuna: 118
Venus: 51, 119, 127, 145
Venus (planet): 51, 119
Vice: 11, 12, 13, 25, 30, 35, 49, 54,
    57, 66, 68, 74, 96, 104, 113, 114
Victory: 50
Vine: 121
Virtue: 11, 12, 20, 25, 31, 35, 49,
    54, 48, 74, 113, 114
Vibration: 23
Vishnu: 25
Vision of Beauty Triumphant: 53,
    59, 100
Vision of God Face to Face: 23
Vision of the Holy Guardian Angel:
    74, 115
Vision of Love: 34, 123
Vision of Power: 43, 121, 104
Vision of Sorrow: 28, 30, 123
Vision of Splendor: 59, 118
Vision of the Harmony of Things:
    47, 121
Vision of the Machinery of the Uni-
    verse: 13, 68, 100, 117
Vision of the Source We Seek: 23,
    124
Vulcan: 122

wand: 65
Water: 74, 145
Water Grade: 104
Westcott, Wynn: 114
Wheel of Life: 34, 68
wheels: 76
Wheels: 23
White Goddess: 53
Willows: 117
Wind in the Willows: 39
Winter: 79
Wisdom: 125
Wisdom God/desses: 125

Witchcraft: 2
Womb of Life: 28

Yah: 23, 124
Yahveh: 23, 124
Yahveh Eloah Va Daath: 49, 120
Yahveh Elohim: 30, 125
Yahveh Tzabaoth: 119
Yesod-Chapter 11: (63-60), 71, 74,
    83, 90, 91, 92, 93, 94, 99, 103,
    104, 108, 109, 117, 129, 136
Yetzirah: 77
Yin and Yang: 31
Yod: 125
yoni: 125
Yorillo: 117

Zeus: 24, 33, 125
Zodiac: 19, 74, 79, 124

STAY IN TOUCH

On the following pages you will find some of the books now available on related subjects. Your book dealer stocks most of these and will stock new titles in the Llewellyn series as they become available. We urge your patronage.

To obtain our full catalog, to keep informed about new titles as they are released and to benefit from informative articles and helpful news, you are invited to write for our bimonthly news magazine/catalog, *Llewellyn's New Worlds of Mind and Spirit*. A sample copy is free, and it will continue coming to you at no cost as long as you are an active mail customer. Or you may subscribe for just $7.00 in the U.S.A. and Canada ($20.00 overseas, first class mail). Many bookstores also have *New Worlds* available to their customers. Ask for it.

Llewellyn's New Worlds of Mind and Spirit
P.O. Box 64383-047, St. Paul, MN 55164-0383, U.S.A.
* * *

TO ORDER BOOKS AND TAPES

If your book dealer does not have the books described, you may order them directly from the publisher by sending full price in U.S. funds, plus $3.00 for postage and handling for orders *under* $10.00; $4.00 for orders *over* $10.00. There are no postage and handling charges for orders over $50.00. Postage and handling rates are subject to change. We ship UPS whenever possible. Delivery guaranteed. Provide your street address as UPS does not deliver to P.O. Boxes. UPS to Canada requires a $50.00 minimum order. Allow 4-6 weeks for delivery. Orders outside the U.S.A. and Canada: Airmail—add retail price of book; add $5.00 for each non-book item (tapes, etc.); add $1.00 per item for surface mail.

FOR GROUP STUDY AND PURCHASE

Because there is a great deal of interest in group discussion and study of the subject matter of this book, we offer a special quantity price to group leaders or agents. Our special quantity price for a minimum order of five copies of *Practical Color Magick* is $20.85 cash-with-order. This price includes postage and handling within the United States. Minnesota residents must add 6.5% sales tax. For additional quantities, please order in multiples of five. For Canadian and foreign orders, add postage and handling charges as above. Credit card (VISA, MasterCard, American Express) orders are accepted. Charge card orders only ($15.00 minimum order) may be phoned in free within the U.S.A. or Canada by dialing 1-800-THE-MOON. For customer service, call 1-612-291-1970. Mail orders to:

LLEWELLYN PUBLICATIONS
P.O. Box 64383-047, St. Paul, MN 55164-0383, U.S.A.

Prices subject to change without notice.

THE WITCHES TAROT
The Witches Qabala, Book II
by Ellen Cannon Reed

In this book Ellen Cannon Reed has further defined the complex, inner workings of the Qabalistic Tree of Life. She brings together the Major and Minor Arcana cards with the Tree of Life to provide readers with a unique insight on the meaning of the Paths on the Tree. Included is a complete section on divination with the Tarot cards, with several layout patterns and explanations clearly presented.

The Major Arcana cards are also keys to Pathworking astral journeys through the Tree of Life. Reed explains Pathworking and gives several examples. An appendix gives a list of correspondences for each of the Paths including the associated Tarot card, Hebrew letter, colors, astrological attribution, animal, gem, and suggested meditation. This book is a valuable addition to the literature of the Tarot and the Qabala.

0-87542-668-9, 320 pgs., 5-1/4 x 8, illus., softcover   **$9.95**

THE WITCHES TAROT DECK
by Ellen Cannon Reed and Martin Cannon

Author Ellen Cannon Reed has created the first Tarot deck specifically for Pagans and Wiccans. Reed, herself a Wiccan High Priestess, developed The Witches Tarot as a way to teach the truths of the Hebrew Kabbalah from a clear and distinctly Pagan point of view. Changes include a Horned One in place of the traditional Devil, a High Priest in place of the old Hierophant, and a Seeker in place of the Hermit. Comes complete with an instruction booklet that tells you what the cards mean and explains how to use the "Celtic Cross" and "Four Seasons" layouts. The gorgeous, detailed paintings by Martin Cannon make this a true combination of new beauty and ancient symbolism. Even many non-pagans have reported excellent results with the cards and appreciate their colorful and timeless beauty.

0-87542-669-7, boxed set: 78 cards with booklet   **$17.95**

THE MIDDLE PILLAR
by Israel Regardie

Between the two outer pillars of the Qabalistic Tree of Life, the extremes of Mercy and Severity, stands the Middle Pillar, signifying one who has achieved equilibrium in his or her own self.

Integration of the human personality is vital to the continuance of creative life. Without it, man lives as an outsider to his own true self. By combining magic and psychology in the Middle Pillar Ritual/Exercise (a magical meditation technique), we bring into balance the opposing elements of the psyche while yet holding within their essence and allowing full expression of man's entire being.

In this book, and with this practice, you will learn to: understand the psyche through its correspondences of the Tree of Life; expand self-awareness, thereby intensifying the inner growth process; activate creative and intuitive potentials; understand the individual thought patterns which control every facet of personal behavior; and regain the sense of balance and peace of mind—the equilibrium—that everyone needs for phsyical and psychic health.

0-87542-658-1, 176 pgs., 5-1/4 x 8, softcover $8.95

A GARDEN OF POMEGRANATES
by Israel Regardie

What is the Tree of Life? It's the ground plan of the Qabalistic system—a set of symbols used since ancient times to study the Universe. The Tree of Life is a geometrical arrangement of ten sephiroth, or spheres, each of which is associated with a different archetypal idea, and 22 paths which connect the spheres.This system of primal correspondences has been found the most efficient plan ever devised to classify and organize the characteristics of the self. Israel Regardie has written one of the best and most lucid introductions to the Qabalah. *A Garden of Pomegranates* combines Regardie's own studies with his notes on the works of Aleister Crowley, A.E. Waite, Eliphas Levi and D.H. Lawrence. No longer is the wisdom of the Qabalah to be held secret! The needs of today place the burden of growth upon each and every person . . . each has to undertake the Path as his or her own responsibility, but every help is given in the most ancient and yet most modern teaching here known to humankind.

0-87542-690-5, 160 pgs., 5-1/4 x 8, softcover $8.95

ARCHETYPES ON THE TREE OF LIFE
The Tarot as Pathwork
by Madonna Compton

The "Tree" is the Kabbalistic Tree of Life, the ageless mystical map to the secrets of the Universe. By working with its 10 circular paths and 22 linear ones, you can find answers to life's most profound questions. By mapping archetypes on the Tree, you can trace mythological and religious themes as well as those symbols that stir the psyche on deep inner levels. It can help you bring out your latent powers and develop your full potential.

Archetypes on the Tree of Life symbolically examines the meanings and uses of the 22 paths based upon their correspondences with the Tarot trumps and Hebrew letters. The first half of the book is a scholarly approach to deciphering the archetypal symbols behind the etiology of the Hebrew letters, names and numbers. The second half enhances creativity and intuition through meditations and exercises that bring the material alive in the reader's subconscious. Along the way, you will investigate the mystical and allegorical interpretaions of the Old and New Testaments and compare these and other mythologies worldwide to the Tarot archetypes.

0-87542-104-0, 336 pgs., 6 x 9, illus., softcover   **$12.95**

SIMPLIFIED MAGIC
A Beginner's Guide to the New Age Qabala
by Ted Andrews

In every person, the qualities essential for accelerating his or her growth and spiritual evolution are innate, but even those who recognize such potentials need an effective means of releasing them. The ancient and mystical Qabala is that means.

Simplified Magic offers a simple understanding of what the Qabala is and how it operates. It provides practical methods and techniques so that the energies and forces within the system and within ourselves can be experienced in a manner that enhances growth and releases our greater potential. A reader knowing absolutely nothing about the Qabala could apply the methods in this book with noticeable success! The Qabala is a system for personal attainment and magic that anyone can learn and put to use in his or her life. The secret is that the main glyph of the Qabala, the Tree of Life, is within you. The Tree of Life is a map to the levels of consciousness, power and magic. By learning the Qabala, you will be able to tap into these levels and bring peace, healing, power, love, light and magic into your life.

0-87542-015-X, 208 pgs., mass market, illus.   **$3.95**

Prices subject to change without notice.

THE LLEWELLYN PRACTICAL GUIDE TO
THE DEVELOPMENT OF PSYCHIC POWERS
by Denning & Phillips

You may not realize it, but you already have the ability to use ESP, astral vision and clairvoyance, divination, dowsing, prophecy, and communication with spirits. Written by two of the most knowledgeable experts in the world of psychic development, this book is a complete course—teaching you, step-by-step, how to develop these powers that actually have been yours since birth. Using the techniques, you will soon be able to move objects at a distance, see into the future, know the thoughts and feelings of another person, find lost objects and locate water using your no-longer latent talents.

Psychic powers are as much a natural ability as any other talent. You'll learn to play with these new skills, working with groups of friends to accomplish things you never would have believed possible before reading this book. The text shows you how to make the equipment you can use, the exercises you can do—many of them at any time, anywhere—and how to use your abilities to change your life and the lives of those close to you. Many of the exercises are presented in forms that can be adapted as games for pleasure and fun, as well as development.

0-87542-191-1, 272 pgs., 5-1/4 x 8, illus., softcover   **$8.95**

THE LLEWELLYN PRACTICAL GUIDE TO
THE MAGICK OF THE TAROT
by Denning & Phillips

"To gain understanding, and control, of your life"—Can anything be more important? To gain insight into the circumstances of your life—the inner causes, the karmic needs, the hidden factors at work—and then to have the power to change your life in order to fulfill your real desires and true will: that's what the techniques taught in this book can do.

Discover the shadows cast ahead by coming events. Yes, this is possible, because it is your DEEP MIND—that part of your psyche, normally beyond your conscious awareness, which is in touch with the World Soul and with your own Higher (and Divine) Self—that perceives the astral shadows of coming events and can communicate them to you through the symbols and images of the ancient and mysterious Tarot cards.

Your Deep Mind has the power to shape those astral shadows—images that are causal to material events—when you learn to communicate your own desires and goals using the Tarot.

0-87542-198-9, 252 pgs., 5-1/4 x 8, illus., softcover   **$8.95**

Prices subject to change without notice.

EARTH POWER
Techniques of Natural Magic
by Scott Cunningham

Magick is the art of working with the forces of Nature to bring about necessar and desired, changes. The forces of Nature—expressed through Earth, Air, Fire and Water—are our "spiritual ancestors" who paved the way for our emergence from the prehistoric seas of creation. Attuning to and working with these energies in magick not only lends you the power to affect changes in your life, it also allows you to sense your own place in the larger scheme of Nature. Using the "Old Ways" enables you to live a better life and to deepen your understanding of the world. The tools and powers of magick are around you, waiting to be grasped and utilized. This book gives you the means to put Magick into your life, shows you how to make and use the tools, and gives you spells for every purpose

0-87542-121-0, 176 pgs., 5-1/4 x 8, illus., softcover   **$8.95**

CIRCLES, GROVES & SANCTUARIES
Sacred Spaces of Today's Pagans
Compiled by Dan & Pauline Campanelli

Pagans and Wiccans have always been secretive people. Even many within the Craft have not been allowed to enter the sacred space of others. But within the pages of *Circles, Groves & Sanctuaries*, you are given the unique opportunity to examine, in intimate detail, the magical places created by Pagans and Witches across the country, around the world and from a wide variety of traditions.

Take guided tours of sacred spaces by the people who created them, and listen as they tell of the secret meanings and magical symbolism of the sometimes strange and always wonderful objects that adorn these places. Learn of their rituals that can be adapted by the most seasoned practitioner or the newest seeker on the hidden path. Become inspired to create your own magical space—indoors or out, large or small.

Accompany an Irish Count on a vision quest that led to the creation of a shrine to Poseidon. Read of the Celtic-speaking Fairies who dwell and practice their arts in Florida, and learn of the logistics of building a wood-henge in suburban New Jersey and a stone circle in the heart of the Bible Belt.

0-87542-108-3, 256 pgs., 7 x 10, 120 photos, softcover   **$12.95**

GROWING THE TREE WITHIN
Patterns of the Unconscious Revealed by the Qabalah
by William Gray

The Qabalah, or Tree of Life, has been the basic genetic pattern of Western esotericism, and it shows us how to make our climb steadily back to Heaven. When we study the Qabalah, open ourselves to it and work with it, we gain wisdom that will illuminate our individual paths to perfection.

Formerly titled *The Talking Tree,* this book presents an exhaustive and systematic analysis of the 22 Paths of the Tree of Life. It includes a comprehensive study of the symbolism of the Tarot cards in which author William Gray presents a viable yet unorthodox method of allocating the Major Arcana to the Paths. Of particular interest is his attempt at reaching a better understanding of the nature of the English alphabet and its correspondence to the Tree of Life.

Gray contends that the "traditional" Tree is a living spirit that needs to be in a continual state of evolution and improvement. It is the duty of all those who love and work with it to cultivate and develop it with every care. This includes both pruning off dead wood and training new growth in the right directions for future fruiting. *Growing the Tree Within* does precisely that.

0-87542-268-3, 468 pgs., 6 x 9, illus., softcover **$14.95**

INVOCATION OF THE GODS
Ancient Egyptian Magic for Today
by Ellen Cannon Reed

Ancient Egypt—*Tamera*—a civilization that exists now only in its ruins—has fascinated people for centuries. Now this mysteriously enchanting subject is brought to life for modern readers in *Invocation of the Gods.* It demonstrates how the gods and goddesses of ancient Egypt can influence and benefit our spiritual and physical lives today through proper invocation and worship.

Ellen Cannon Reed presents a thought-provoking blend of ancient Egyptian deities with modern Wicca. *Invocation of the Gods* touches on the heart of the Craft: the Gods, and love and service to them.

If you have read any of the books by Egyptologists and found them unsatisfying because they were about "other people's" religion, if you have looked at the ancient writings and longed to understand them better, if you have wanted to include the gods of Egypt and their magic in your own ritual practice, *Invocation of the Gods* will be of immense value to you.

0-87542-667-0, 240 pgs., 6 x 9, illus., softcover **$12.95**

Prices subject to change without notice.

THE MAGICAL PHILOSOPHY, VOLUME 2
The Sword and the Serpent
by Denning & Phillips
This is the comprehensive guide to the Magical Qabalah, with extensive correspondences as well as the techniques for activating the centers, use of images and the psychology of attainment.

In this volume, histories from contemporary life, together with references to the works of mystics, poets, artists, philosophers and authorities in psychology are cited to illustrate the action and interaction of the functions of the psyche as identified in Qabalistic teaching.

The real meaning of adepthood is clearly set forth: in relation to this, frequent enigmas of occult literature such as the Abyss, the Knowledge and Conversation of the Holy Guardian Angel, and the supernal attainments are presented in their true meaning and significance. The natural dignity and potential of life in this world is your birthright. In this volume, its splendor and power are made unmistakably manifest.
0-87542-197-0, 540 pgs., 6 x 9, illus., softcover   **$15.00**

GODWIN'S CABALISTIC ENCYCLOPEDIA
A Complete Guide to Cabalistic Magick
by David Godwin
This is the most complete correlation of Hebrew and English ideas ever offered. It is a dictionary of Cabalism arranged, with definitions, alphabetically in Hebrew and numerically. With this book, the practicing Cabalist or student no longer needs access to a large number of books on mysticism, magic and the occult in order to trace down the basic meanings, Hebrew spellings, and enumerations of the hundreds of terms, words, and names.

This book includes: all of the two-letter root words found in Biblical Hebrew, the many names of God, the planets, the astrological signs, numerous angels, the Shem ha-Mephorash, the Spirits of the *Goetia*, the correspondences of the 32 Paths, a comparison of the Tarot and the Cabala, a guide to Hebrew pronunciation, and a complete edition of Aleister Crowley's valuable book *Sepher Sephiroth*.

Here is a book that is a must for the shelf of all magicians, Cabalists, astrologers, Tarot students, Thelemites, and those with any interest at all in the spiritual aspects of our universe.
0-87542-292-6, 528 pgs., 6 x 9, softcover   **$15.00**

Prices subject to change without notice.

WICCA
A Guide for the Solitary Practitioner
by Scott Cunningham

Wicca is a book of life, and how to live magically, spiritually, and wholly attuned with Nature. Cunningham presents Wicca as it is today: a gentle, Earth-oriented religion dedicated to the Goddess and God. This book fulfills a need for a practical guide to solitary Wicca—a need which no previous book has fulfilled. Here is a positive, practical introduction to the religion of Wicca, designed so that any interested person can learn to practice the religion alone anywhere in the world. It presents Wicca honestly and clearly and shows that Wicca is a vital, satisfying part of twentieth century life.

This book presents the theory and practice of Wicca from an individual's perspective. Based on the author's nearly two decades of Wiccan practice, it presents an eclectic picture of various aspects of this religion. Exercises designed to develop magical proficiency, a self-dedication ritual, herb, crystal and rune magic, recipes for Sabbat feasts are included in this excellent book.

0-87542-118-0, 240 pgs., 6 x 9, illus., softcover $9.95

BUCKLAND'S COMPLETE BOOK OF WITCHCRAFT
by Raymond Buckland

Here is the most complete resource to the study and practice of modern, non-denominational Wicca. This is a lavishly illustrated, self-study course for the solitary or group. Included are rituals; exercises for developing psychic talents; information on all major "sects" of the Craft; sections on tools, beliefs, dreams, meditations, divination, herbal lore, healing, ritual clothing and more. This book unites theory and practice into a comprehensive course designed to help you develop into a practicing Witch. Written by Ray Buckland, a very famous and respected authority on Witchcraft who first came public with the Old Religion in the United States, this book is large format with workbook-type exercises and full of music and chants.

Never before has so much information on the Craft of the Wise been collected in one place. Traditionally, there are three degrees of advancement in most Wiccan traditions. When you have completed studying this book, you will be the equivalent of a Third-Degree Witch. Even those who have practiced Wicca for years find useful information in this book, and many covens are using this for their textbook. If you want to become a Witch, or if you merely want to find out what Witchcraft is really about, you will find no better book than this.

0-87542-050-8, 272 pgs., 8-1/2 x 11, illus., softcover $14.95

Prices subject to change without notice.

CUNNINGHAM'S ENCYCLOPEDIA OF CRYSTAL, GEM & METAL MAGIC
by Scott Cunningham

Here you will find the most complete information anywhere on the magical qualities of more than 100 crystals and gemstones as well as several metals. The information for each crystal, gem or metal includes: its related energy, planetary rulership, magical element, deities, Tarot card, and the magical powers that each is believed to possess. Also included is a complete description of their uses for magical purposes. The classic on the subject.

0-87542-126-1, 240 pgs., 6 x 9, illus., color plates   **$12.95**

CUNNINGHAM'S ENCYCLOPEDIA OF MAGICAL HERBS
by Scott Cunningham

This is the most comprehensive source of herbal data for magical uses ever printed! Almost all of the over 400 herbs are illustrated, making this a great source for herb identification. For each herb you will also find: magical properties, planetary rulerships, genders, associated deities, folk and Latin names and much more. To make this book even easier to use, it contains a folk name cross reference, and all of the herbs are fully indexed. There is also a large annotated bibliography, and a list of mail order suppliers so you can find the books and herbs you need.

Like all of Cunningham's books, this one does not require you to use complicated rituals or expensive magical paraphernalia. Instead, it shares with you the intrinsic powers of the herbs. Thus, you will be able to discover which herbs, by their very nature, can be used for luck, love, success, money, divination, astral projection, safety, psychic self-defense and much more.

Besides being interesting and educational it is also fun, and fully illustrated with unusual woodcuts from old herbals. This book has rapidly become the classic in its field. It enhances books such as *777* and is a must for all Wiccans.

0-87542-122-9, 336 pgs., 6 x 9, illus.   **$12.95**

THE BOOK OF GODDESSES & HEROINES
by Patricia Monaghan

The Book of Goddesses & Heroines is a historical landmark, a must for everyone interested in Goddesses and Goddess worship. It is not an effort to trivialize the beliefs of matriarchal cultures. It is not a collection of Goddess descriptions penned by biased male historians throughout the ages. It is the complete, non-biased account of Goddesses of every cultural and geographic area, including African, Egyptian, Japanese, Korean, Persian, Australian, Pacific, Latin American, British, Irish, Scottish, Welsh, Chinese, Greek, Icelandic, Italian, Finnish, German, Scandinavian, Indian, Tibetan, Mesopotamian, North American, Semitic and Slavic Goddesses!

Envisioning herself as a woman who might have revered each of these Goddesses, Patricia Monaghan has done away with language that referred to the deities in relation to their male counterparts, as well as with culturally relative terms such as "married" or "fertility cult." The beliefs of the cultures and the attributes of the Goddesses have been left intact.

Plus, this book has a new, complete index. If you are more concerned about finding a Goddess of war than you are a Goddess of a given country, this index will lead you to the right page. This is especially useful for anyone seeking to do Goddess rituals. Your work will be twice as efficient and effective with this detailed and easy-to-use book.

0-87542-573-9, 456 pgs., 6 x 9, photos, softcover **$17.95**

YEAR OF MOONS, SEASON OF TREES
Mysteries and Rites of Celtic Tree Magick
by Pattalee Glass-Koentop

Many of you are drawn to Wicca, or the Craft, but do not have teachers or like-minded people around to show you how the religion is practiced. *Year of Moons, Season of Trees* serves as that teacher and as a sourcebook. Most Witchcraft in America comes from or has been influenced by that of the British Isles. The Druidic sacred trees native to that culture are the focus of this book. The essence, imagery and mythology behind the trees and seasons is vividly portrayed. The author provides the how-to for rituals celebrating Nature through its Moons, its Seasons and Months of Trees. Here is the history, the lore of each tree, the rituals of Temple Workings, songs and chants, even recipes that complete these celebrations. Also included are Ogham correspondence charts and descriptive lists of solar and lunar trees.

0-87542-269-1, 264 pgs., 7 x 10, illus., softcover **$14.95**

Prices subject to change without notice.

THE LLEWELLYN ANNUALS

Llewellyn's MOON SIGN BOOK: Over 400 pages of valuable information on gardening, fishing, weather, stock market forecasts, horoscopes, planting dates, and instructions for finding the best date to do just about anything! Articles by prominent forecasters and writers in the fields of gardening, astrology, politics, economics and cycles. This special almanac, different from any other, has been published annually since 1906. It's fun, informative and has been a great help to millions in their daily planning. **State year $4.95**

Llewellyn's SUN SIGN BOOK: Your personal horoscope for the entire year! All 12 signs are included in one handy book. Also included are forecasts, special feature articles, and an action guide for each sign. Monthly horoscopes are written by Gloria Star, author of *Optimum Child*, for your personal Sun Sign and there are articles on a variety of subjects written by well-known astrologers from around the country. Much more than just a horoscope guide! Entertaining and fun the year around. **State year $4.95**

Llewellyn's DAILY PLANETARY GUIDE: Includes all of the major daily aspects plus their exact times in Eastern and Pacific time zones, lunar phases, signs and voids plus their times, planetary motion, a monthly ephemeris, sunrise and sunset tables, special articles on the planets, signs, aspects, a business guide, planetary hours, rulerships, and much more. Large 5-1/4 x 8 format for more writing space, spiral bound to lay flat, address and phone listings, time-zone conversion chart and blank horoscope chart. **State year $6.95**

Llewellyn's ASTROLOGICAL CALENDAR: Large wall calendar of 48 pages. Beautiful full-color cover and paintings. Includes feature articles by famous astrologers, and complete introductory information on astrology. It also contains a Lunar Gardening Guide, celestial phenomena, a blank horoscope chart, and monthly date pages which include aspects, Moon phases, signs and voids, planetary motion, an ephemeris, personal forecasts, planting and fishing dates, and more. 10 x 13 size. Set in Central time, with fold-down conversion table for other time zones worldwide. **State year $9.95**

Llewellyn's MAGICAL ALMANAC: This beautifully illustrated almanac explores traditional earth religions and folklore while focusing on magical myths. Each month is summarized in a two-page format with information that includes the phases of the moon, festivals and rites for the month, as well as detailed magical advice. This is an indispensable guide is for anyone who is interested in planning rituals, spells and other magical advice. It features writing by some of the most prominent authors in the field. **State year $7.95**

Prices subject to change without notice.